## DATE DUE

| | | | |
|---|---|---|---|
| | | | |
| | | | |
| | | | |
| | | | |
| | | | |
| | | | |
| | | | |
| | | | |
| | | | |
| | | | |
| | | | |
| | | | |
| | | | |
| | | | |
| | | | |
| | | | |
| | | | |
| | | | |

HIGHSMITH 45-220

# Columbia University

# Contributions to Education

## Teachers College Series

## No. 781

# AMS PRESS
### NEW YORK

# SPELLING AS A SECONDARY LEARNING

THE EXTENSION OF SPELLING VOCABULARIES
WITH DIFFERENT METHODS OF ORGANIZING
AND TEACHING THE SOCIAL STUDIES

By

## I. KEITH TYLER

SUBMITTED IN PARTIAL FULFILLMENT OF THE REQUIREMENTS FOR
THE DEGREE OF DOCTOR OF PHILOSOPHY IN THE FACULTY OF
PHILOSOPHY, COLUMBIA UNIVERSITY

*Published with the Approval of
Professor Herbert B. Bruner, Sponsor*

BUREAU OF PUBLICATIONS
Teachers College, Columbia University
NEW YORK
1939

**Library of Congress Cataloging in Publication Data**

Tyler, I. Keith, 1905-
    Spelling as a secondary learning.

    Reprint of the 1939 ed., issued in series:  Teachers
College, Columbia University.  Contributions to educa-
tion, no. 781.
        Originally presented as the author's thesis, Columbia.
        Bibliography:  p.
        1.  English language--Orthography and spelling.
2.  Vocabulary.  3.  Social sciences--Study and teaching.
I.  Title.  II.  Series:  Columbia University.  Teachers
College.  Contributions to education, no. 781.
LB1574.T9  1972        372.6'32        79-177688

ISBN 0-404-55781-3

Reprinted by Special Arrangement with Teachers
College Press, New York, New York

From the edition of 1939, New York
First AMS edition published in 1972
Manufactured in the United States

AMS PRESS, INC.
NEW YORK, N. Y.    10003

# Acknowledgments

THE author is especially indebted to his sponsor, Professor Herbert B. Bruner, of Teachers College, for his constant encouragement, and for arranging the field experience out of which this study grew. Grateful appreciation is expressed to Professor Arthur I. Gates, of Teachers College, for helpful criticisms and suggestions, and to Professors Louis Raths, of Ohio State University, and R. W. Tyler, of the University of Chicago, for suggestions regarding statistical treatment.

The study would not have been possible without the interested, active cooperation of Mr. Charles L. Kopp, Miss Lillian Compton, and Miss Katharine Healy, school officials in Maryland, who arranged for the participation of the schools in the study and gave invaluable help in carrying out the experiment.

Tribute also should be paid to Miss Anna Crosser and Mrs. Alice Beighley for endless hours of clerical work and statistical computation.

Finally, special mention should be made of the inexhaustible patience of my wife, Margaret, and of Dean Thomas E. Benner and Professor W. W. Charters.

I. K. T.

# Contents

# Tables

# I

## Introduction—Origin and Importance

ONE of the most significant developments in American educational practice is its reorientation from a preoccupation with skills and information to a concern with the whole range of changes in boys and girls as a result of the educational experience. This shift in focus to the wider aspects of learning has unquestionably been influenced by educational philosophy which in turn has been modified by developments in psychology and physiology. But the full force of the change did not become manifest until the rise of the so-called progressive schools which attempted seriously to concern themselves with the "whole child" and with education as the process by which the environment interacts with the organism to produce changes in the latter. Education as "experience" became the keynote of these new schools. While many aspects of the programs of these schools were frowned upon by the more traditional educators, there was an increasing acceptance of some of the more fundamental principles which were involved in the experiments. One of the most important of these was the recognition that learning involves much more than the acquisition of facts and narrow skills.

*Secondary Learning.* Children learn not only those things for which a learning activity is primarily arranged, but many other things as well, during the course of the activity. The term "secondary learning" may be applied to these more or less unforeseen changes which take place in boys and girls as a result of school experiences because such learning occurs secondarily to the attainment of other primary objectives. This is not to imply that such learning is not important, but rather to emphasize that its attainment is not aimed at directly. Some kind of secondary learning is an inevitable accompaniment of every educational experience. Some things, such as learning to read or to spell, may be secondary learnings in one activity, and primary learnings in another educational activity.

These secondary learnings may be noted in relation to any given educational situation. A good teacher is conscious that while primary attention is centered upon learning the particular skills involved in a phase of long division, for example, the children are simultaneously acquiring attitudes toward such arithmetical processes, adding words to their vocabulary, "fixing" habits of posture, learning means of securing attention from their fellows, and the like. Instruction attempts to take into account these secondary learnings by careful control not only of the factors directly associated with the primary goals but of the more incidental factors also. Thus, a teacher is concerned with the attitudes which children develop toward war as a means of settling disputes even when the primary purposes of the teaching may be in terms of certain facts relating to the Civil War. The inclusion of so-called recreational reading as a part of the elementary school program is primarily a means of improving the child's reading ability and widening his acquaintance with good reading materials, but it results also in extending his vocabulary and giving him background in such varying fields as science, the social studies, and art. Learnings are secondary, then, when they are not the primary goals of the planned educational experience. They may or may not be recognized by teachers.

The variety of these extra learnings may be noted by a casual analysis of even the simplest learning situation. Learning to spell a list of ten words seems a fairly easy task as compared with the difficulty of developing an adequate understanding of the complex forces and movements which led to the American Civil War. Yet in the spelling situation we may distinguish several types of possible learnings. First, there is the primary one of acquiring the ability to write without error and in proper sequence the letters making up the words as they are dictated by the teacher. Second, there are learnings not directly aimed at, but associated with the subject. These may or may not be desirable. Thus, in relation to spelling, a study by Carroll[1] shows that bright children tend to generalize, particularly in phonetics, in spelling unfamiliar words. The phonetic rules thus formulated are, however, so frequently violated by English words as often to make this very tendency to generalize a handicap in learning to spell. Third, there are learnings in associated fields. In the spelling lesson, for example, the child may be acquiring new word meanings, he may be extending his speaking and writing vocabulary as well as his spelling vocabulary, and an improvement in word usage may be an indirect result of using some of the spelling words in sentences. Fourth, there is the acquisition of habits of work and study—learning to concentrate attention upon the spelling drill in order to shorten the time required for "fixing" the words, learning to use a dictionary, and the like. And lastly, there are the changes in attitudes which accompany any life situation. These may be reenforcements of previously acquired attitudes; they may be newly-learned likes or dislikes for the subject, the teacher; or they may be associated with any of the other elements in the total situation.

Every learning situation, then, results to a greater or lesser degree in each of these types of learning. The importance placed upon a particular type, however, depends upon such factors as what is being taught, the situation in which it is taught, and the point of view dominating those concerned with the situation.

Emphasis in the past was largely upon the primary learnings. To be sure, when the triviality or unimportance of some of these was made clear, the defenders of the status quo fell back upon assumed learnings of the fourth type. They enlarged upon the benefits of a "disciplined mind" or of the "power of concentration" which were presumed to be inherent accompaniments to the mastery of dull content. But on the whole the classroom teacher centered his activity and that of his pupils upon the attainment of the specific facts and skills which were the recognized primary goals of the subject.

In modern education, however, there is a clear recognition of the complex outcomes of the learning process. Goals are set up not only in terms of facts and skills but also in relation to generaliza-

[1] Herbert Allen Carroll, *Generalization of Bright and Dull Children; A Comparative Study with Special Reference to Spelling.* Bureau of Publications, Teachers College, Columbia University, New York, 1930.

tions and inferences which are built up over longer periods of time. Similarly, subject boundaries tend to be disregarded and outcomes are thought of in relation to associated fields as well as to the immediate area under consideration. Likewise, habits of work and study, and attitudes toward persons and problems are recognized as important. Indeed, many progressive schools defend their instructional practices largely in terms of these latter goals. Hence, secondary learning looms ever larger as an important element in the educational process.

*Evaluating Secondary Learning.* With the increased recognition of the importance of secondary learning, and even more with the attention given to such learning in the educational process, has come the need for adequate evidence that such learning actually takes place, and of the conditions under which it occurs. Careful research studies seeking such evidence are now beginning to appear. But the difficulties of measurement of outcomes as intangible as attitudes or habits of work have made advance in this field very slow. That such validating research is necessary few would deny.

Further progress in many areas is dependent upon reliable evidence of secondary learning. Most of the comparative studies of teaching methods and of such factors as class size have been based upon the results of measures of facts and skills. The few early attempts that were made to compare the outcomes of instruction in progressive schools with those in traditional schools were based almost entirely upon these same inadequate measures. Yet in many cases the outcomes which were most likely to be influenced by the particular elements being studied were not those pertaining to the acquisition of facts and simple skills but rather the very habits of work and attitudes for which no adequate measures existed at that time.

More recently, however, a number of comparative studies have appeared based upon an evaluation of the achievement of other important objectives. Wrightstone,[2] for example, compared con-

[2] J. Wayne Wrightstone, *Appraisal of Newer Elementary School Practices.* Bureau of Publications, Teachers College, Columbia University, New York, 1938.
J. Wayne Wrightstone, *Appraisal of Experimental High School Practices.* Bureau of Publications, Teachers College, Columbia University, New York, 1936.

ventional and experimental elementary schools on the basis of the achievement of the children in relation to six objectives: (1) to understand and practice desirable social relationships; (2) to discover and develop individual aptitudes; (3) to cultivate powers of critical thinking; (4) to appreciate worth-while activities; (5) to gain command of the common integrating knowledge and skills; and (6) to build sound physical and mental health. He concludes that "most of the indexes are favorable to the experimental schools" included in the study.

Similarly, in comparing conventional and experimental high schools on the basis of certain intellectual factors, dynamic factors, and social performance factors, he found evidence of equal or superior achievement for the experimental schools.

Both of these studies extended evaluation beyond the traditional subject matter to include learnings of a broader and more inclusive type. Other procedures in evaluating broad outcomes of learning are described in a special issue of *Educational Method* devoted to "The Problem of Evaluation."[3]

The necessity of adequate evaluation of such incidental learnings becomes most striking when the results of an experimental reorganization of secondary education are being compared with the outcomes from the more traditional educational program. Thus, the Commission on the Relation of School and College of the Progressive Education Association is engaged in "the task of developing adequate ways of measuring and evaluating the results"[4] of an eight-year experiment in which thirty secondary schools have been freed from the customary college requirements in order to attempt the improvement of their programs. Such an evaluation is not to be confined to types of learnings which may already be satisfactorily measured by existing tests. It will so far as possible be based upon the agreed objectives of the several schools.

These objectives will indicate the variety of aspects of pupil development which needs to be considered in a satisfactory program of evaluation. This statement of purposes will probably include statements of

[3] "The Problem of Evaluation," Special Issue of *Educational Method*, XV (May, 1936).

[4] Wilford M. Aikin, "The Purpose of the Eight-Year Experimental Study," *Educational Record* (January, 1935), p. 15.

certain understandings to be developed, certain attitudes to be acquired, certain skills and habits to be realized.[5]

A much simpler type of secondary learning, however, still needs additional study. More investigation is needed of the effects upon abilities in associated fields of the activity planned to further growth in a particular field. That the wide reading and elementary research which accompanies work in such subjects as the social studies "is the main means of extending, refining, and perfecting reading tastes and techniques" has been indicated by Gates.[6] Similarly, a program which encourages extensive reading in the field of science may be expected to improve the child's social studies background because of the interrelationships which are so frequent in the two areas. Most of the subjects in the elementary school have certain elements in common among them so that achievement in any one subject may be expected to influence learning in others. Frequently, however, teaching proceeds as though such secondary learnings did not exist.

*Selection of the Problem.* A recognition of the possibility of secondary learning taking place in the field of social studies in the elementary school led to the setting up of the present problem. Obviously all of the possible secondary learnings could not be investigated without an exhaustive and comprehensive study, beyond the resources of the writer. But an attempt to investigate the effect of the teaching of three social studies units in the sixth grade in a certain school system upon a small area of possible secondary learning was feasible. More extended investigation could wait upon the outcome of the present study.

The area chosen had, necessarily, to be both limited in scope and of a sort which could be measured objectively, taking into consideration present inadequacies of evaluation. The most likely field for investigation which met these qualifications was that of spelling. It seemed probable that social studies activity would affect spelling since the field involves almost continuous contact with

[5] Ralph W. Tyler, "Evaluation: a Challenge to Progressive Education," *Educational Research Bulletin:* XIV (January 16, 1935), p. 13.

[6] Arthur I. Gates, *Reading for Public School Administrators.* Bureau of Publications, Teachers College, Columbia University, New York, 1931.

words and ideas. The problem, therefore, was limited to the effect of these social studies units upon children's ability to spell.

A different angle of attack was taken after considerable study because of the writer's interest in certain problems which seemed to him to be crucial in relation to the teaching of spelling. These problems concerned the words to be taught in school. While individual differences among children are recognized so far as rate of learning is concerned, little attention is paid to differences among children in the words they need to know how to spell. To be sure, it is probably true that the two or three thousand commonest words are sufficiently important to all children to require their teaching as one of the "fundamentals" of the elementary school. There has, indeed, been much research carried on in an attempt to discover what these common words are. There have been studies both of adult and children's writings. But with the exception of the studies of the special vocabulary involved in the writings of certain professional groups, all have been oriented in terms of the words common to all adults or all children. Individual differences have had little consideration.

Thompson, in his study, *The Effectiveness of Modern Spelling Instruction,* shows clearly that individual differences enter into the determination of the most commonly used words. He says :[7]

. . . At this point, it may be suggested that the concept of the "most commonly used words" involves many difficulties. Sociologically, no doubt, it should be possible to determine the 5,000 or 10,000 most commonly used words for a social group or even a nation. But there is also a psychological aspect to the matter. Would the individual variation in the use of words by members of the group be so small that each individual list of "most commonly used words" would substantially agree with each of the other individual lists? Would the lists, say, of 75 per cent of the members of a group, be substantially the same? . . .
. . . When the wide range of material which Horn used to compile the Commonwealth List is considered and when it seems probable that the great majority of pupils will not need to write more than two or three different types of material, the probability that one individual's list of most frequently used words beyond the first 1,000 will approximate another's must be taken as remote. Of course, the inclusion of so many different sorts of written materials for compilation makes for

[7] Robert S. Thompson, *The Effectiveness of Modern Spelling Instruction.* p. 18. Bureau of Publications, Teachers College, Columbia University, New York, 1930.

sociological validity of Horn's lists. On the other hand, the fact that it was necessary to use so many different kinds of writing to get a valid list indicates that the list cannot be an individual one.

But what of these hundreds of additional words which each child uses over and above the "common" ones? These differ from one child to another, apparently, according to the differing interests and abilities. If we accept as a major objective in spelling the ability to spell the words the child needs to use in his written expression, the problem of where and how such an individual spelling vocabulary is to be acquired becomes of major importance. Is it possible that such a spelling vocabulary is being acquired secondarily through the activity of the child in following his broad interests in the social studies? Is it possible to discover the effect of certain definite social studies units upon the extent of the child's spelling vocabulary? Such questions centered the attack of the writer upon these "interest" words, the "unusual" words peculiar to the unit which the child might be expected to acquire. Our problem becomes, then, not to determine whether the child has mastered a few more of the commonest words with which he comes into contact in practically any activity involving words, but rather to determine whether he has acquired the ability to spell a special group of words which are associated with the unit. If so, then a definite lead is established as to where children may be expected to enlarge their spelling vocabularies. The problem thus centered upon the acquiring of a specialized spelling vocabulary.

Taking another aspect of the problem, let us examine more closely the claims of social studies as a single subject which cuts across several fields compared with similar subject matter taught more in isolation. It has been assumed that one of the major values of the teaching of social studies as a single subject as opposed to the teaching of history, geography, and civics separately has been that the former arrangement is more natural, that it permits to a greater degree the following of children's interests. Social studies, too, as a unified subject is usually taught by the unit plan which makes possible a wider provision for individual differences than does the separate teaching of history, geography, and civics. These subjects, too, are often taught in units, but the subject matter approach is still the more common. Both of these claims would seem to make possible a larger amount of secondary learning of this specialized spelling, if such learning actually took place. So viewed, it became necessary to enlarge the problem so as to investigate the comparative effects of the teaching of social studies as a single subject and of history and geography, separately, upon the secondary learning of the specialized spelling.

With the central problem thus outlined, a host of subsidiary but important questions arose. If this type of learning takes place, what bearing has the intelligence of the child upon the process? What is the relationship of the child's reading ability and his secondary learning of spelling of this type? Does the child who already has a large spelling vocabulary acquire more or fewer words than the child with a small spelling vocabulary? These and many other questions were carefully considered as the problem was outlined and the experimental procedure arranged.

*Statement of the Problem.* The central problem then may be stated as follows: To discover the relationship of the teaching of certain units in social studies and of the teaching of history and geography separately, to the ability of children to spell words peculiar to the units or subjects.

Additional subsidiary questions to be answered are:

1. With which type of subject matter organization is there the greater increase in the child's spelling vocabulary, separate subject organization or a unified social studies approach?

2. Which of the three units shows the greatest effect?

3. What is the relationship between original scores in the test of unusual words and on a standardized spelling test based on common words?

4. What is the relationship between original scores in the test of unusual words and gains made during the experiment?

5. What is the relationship between scores on a standardized spelling test and the gains made?

6. What is the relationship between intelligence scores and original scores on the spelling test?

7. What is the relation between intelligence and gains?

8. What is the relation between reading ability and original scores?

9. What is the relationship between reading ability and gains?

10. What is the relationship between scores in geography and history and original scores in the special spelling test?

11. What is the relationship between scores in geography and history and gains?

# II

## Plan, Setting, and Limitations of the Study

IN ORDER to discover the effects of teaching designated social studies units and of the separate teaching of history and geography upon the ability of children to spell words peculiar to the units or subjects it was necessary to undertake an experimental study. The conditions of such careful experimentation were clear: the groups of children exposed to the various experimental situations must be comparable in all ways which might have significance to the study; their status with regard to the factor being investigated must be measured at the beginning and again at the end of the study; the conditions of learning must be comparable in all important respects except for the experimental factor; the time element must be equal for the several groups; and there must be a clear-cut differentiation from one group to another with regard to the one changing factor so that the differences in results from group to group will represent the effect of the one changed factor only.

*Plan of the Study.* The plan, then, was to select two comparable school situations, roughly equal in size, social and economic status, quality of teaching, and the like. In one of these situations the separate teaching of history and geography from textbooks would be characteristic, while in the other the social studies would be taught as a unified subject organized about units aimed to appeal as closely as possible to the interests of children. Furthermore, within the school system in which social studies were taught as a single subject, it was necessary that the units be sufficiently long and comprehensive so that each unit might result in measurable change. In order to make possible comparisons of one unit with another, the children in the social studies situation would need again to be divided into comparable groups, each group being exposed to the units in a different order so that the effects of each might be segregated.

Data for each child based upon his status at the time of beginning the experiment would be necessary. These would include sex, chronological age, intelligence test score, and measures of achievement in a standardized spelling test, a reading test, a test of language and literature, and a test of history and geography. In addition to this information regarding the status of the child there would, of course, need to be a measure of the ability of the child to spell the words with which he would be coming in contact in the course of the experimental study. For this purpose a special test would need to be constructed based upon the courses of study and the materials of instruction for the various units and subjects.[1] This special spelling test would have to be administered at the beginning of the experiment, at the close of the first unit period, and again at the end of the entire project.

*Setting of the Study.* Two counties in Maryland were chosen as the locale of the study. Both include one principal city in which are centered industrial enterprises which furnish employment for a good share of the people. While Maryland is, strictly speaking, a Southern state, yet these cities are industrial and have many Northern characteristics. In addition to the urban center, each county has several smaller towns and a considerable rural population. Life in town and country is rather barren and meager because of the general depressed condition of agriculture and the geographical features of the districts which are none too favorable to the raising of crops. The two counties are located in the Allegheny Mountains, so that much of the land is extremely hilly. Among the mountains, however, are gentle valleys where agriculture is carried on. Rainfall is plentiful, but much of the soil is either worn out or in poor condition. A network of paved roads throughout the district gives the farm population easy access to the towns and cities so that the farmer by no means is isolated.

[1] See Chapter III for a detailed description of the method used in the construction of this test.

While a few moderately wealthy persons live in each county, the major portion of the population is made up of farm and industrial laborers and a lower middle class whose livelihood depends upon them. The standard of living for the laboring class is below that of similar cities in the North and the income of professional and middle class workers is likewise not up to Northern levels. Otherwise, however, the counties may be said to be fairly typical, and may be duplicated in many places throughout the United States.

The schools of these two counties, in common with those of the entire state except for the city of Baltimore, are organized under a county unit plan. Under this system the county is a single unit of administration, with all schools, rural, town, and city, coming under the same supervisory and administrative personnel. In both counties are one- and two-room rural schools (which are not included in this project), town schools, and city schools. The town and city schools include a number of "consolidated" schools containing rural pupils transported from their farm homes by an elaborate system of school buses. The salaries and training of the teachers are approximately equal since the salary scale and the standards of training are fixed by legislative enactment. State school supervisors rated the level of instruction as being comparable in the two situations.[2] One of the counties taught history and geography as separate subjects while in the other social studies was a unified subject and instruction centered around large units. The latter county will be designated hereafter as County A while the county in which history and geography were separately taught will be designated as County B.

The sixth grade of the two school systems was selected as the level upon which to carry on the experiment. Children in this grade had, for the most part, mastered the mechanics of reading sufficiently to make much use of books and other reading materials and were able to write with relative ease and to spell the commonest words without great difficulty. It seemed reasonable to believe that if there were secondary learning of spelling it would be

[2] The teachers in County A. had participated for two years in a county-wide plan of curriculum revision. This probably gives them an advantage over the teachers in County B in spite of the general ratings.

most apt to occur at the level at which activity involving spelling was frequent and easy. In this grade, too, the units in County A were comprehensive enough to meet the requirements. There were three units, each arranged to consume five weeks, which would lend themselves conveniently to the mechanical requirements of the experiment. The history and geography scheduled to be taught in County B during the same period likewise covered a convenient block of subject matter.

The three units selected in County A were as follows:

1. The Influence of Cotton upon the Development of Our Country.
2. Domesticated Animals—A Factor in the Standard of Living.
3. The Cereal Grains—An Important Factor in Determining Types of Civilization.

Each covered subject matter from history, geography, and other fields which had relevancy to the central theme of the unit. The three units involved pupil activities of wide variety, including extensive reading in many books, magazines, and pamphlets. The units were organized about a central understanding or "theme" which was the central focus of the unit. Activities and subject matter given in the course of study were selected upon the basis of their promise in developing in the boys and girls the central understanding which was the chief goal of each unit. The whole scheme of units for the various grades was arranged so that instruction in the social studies developed a progressive understanding of five major themes which were supposed to be key concepts in understanding human development and history.[3]

In County B the course of study over the experimental period involved a study of the history of Greece and Rome as a part of what is termed "American beginnings in Europe" and the geography of France, Germany, and Russia as a part of a study of the geography of Europe. The course of study itself consisted of short mimeographed outlines of the subject matter to be covered.

---

[3] A more complete description of the units and instructional materials will be found in Chapter IV.

The study was undertaken during the second semester of the school year 1930-31. The experimental period covered the fifteen school weeks from March second to June twelfth.

*Limitations of the Study.* From the plan of the study and the setting in which it was undertaken certain limitations may readily be noted. Briefly summarized these are:

1. The study was limited to that aspect of secondary learning from the teaching of social studies which involves the ability to spell selected words. It is obvious that the study will prove nothing about other types of secondary learning, though if such learning is found in relation to spelling, it will raise fundamental questions about other types of learning which occur incidentally to the attainment of primary objectives in various subjects.

2. The selected words upon which the study was based are all specialized words; i.e., they do not occur in the first three thousand commonest words as given in Thorndike's word list.[4] The study was concerned with discovering some evidence as to the way in which a child's extra spelling vocabulary was acquired, not as to whether his social studies experience improved his spelling of the common words.[5]

3. The study was limited to the immediate effects rather than the residual effects after the lapse of considerable time. The experiment covered fifteen school weeks, and the findings are based on the results at the close of the experiment. Whether or not these effects were lasting the study does not presume to say.

4. The study was limited to secondary learning. The instructions given to the teachers were such as to discourage any direct teaching of these specialized words. Whether such words might be economically learned by being directly taught in connection with their setting in the social studies was not determined.

[4] Edward L. Thorndike, *The Teacher's Word Book.* Bureau of Publications, Teachers College, Columbia University, New York, 1921.

[5] At the time this study was projected an intensive study of the effect of social studies units on children's ability to spell the common words was planned by an associate of the writer. The latter study, however, has not yet been carried out.

# III

## Construction of the Spelling Test

THE success of this entire study of secondary learning of spelling depended very largely upon the adequacy of the instrument by which this secondary learning was to be detected and measured. Obviously the device used had to be set up in terms of the words with which the children might be expected to come in contact. Since the experiment was not an attempt to measure the "level" of spelling ability, no previously prepared standardized test would suffice. Rather was it a study of the secondary learning of the spelling of words which were frequently encountered in the units and subjects which were the center of the children's learning activities. Consequently, the test would necessarily have to be constructed in terms of these units and subjects.

*Sources of the Words.* It seemed reasonable to believe, therefore, that the children would come into contact with new words which were peculiar to the units and subjects studied in the following sources; namely, (1) the textbooks or principal reference books read by most of the pupils; (2) the reference books, magazines, and pamphlets in which supplementary reading was done; (3) the stories or information which the teacher would supply; and (4) the first-hand contact with life situations involving the subject of study, such as in excursions. Another source was also possible and that was the encounter with such words in discussing the subject with their parents or others in the community. Thus, conceivably, the cotton unit which involved a study of the War between the States might lead to much discussion and argument at home in which the child would learn many words with which he was not previously acquainted, though he would probably not need to be able to spell such words. The likelihood, however, was that such conversations would be brought into the school activity in such a way that the teacher and the class would have an opportunity of noting the bearing of such words on the class work. In case such words were important in the study, it would be likely that the teacher would include them in the regular sources mentioned.

*Techniques of Selection.* The procedure used in selecting the words which made up the special spelling test consisted of the eight steps listed below. A detailed description of each step follows the list. The steps were:

1. Obtaining from the teachers lists of words peculiar to the units.
2. Having former pupils write compositions on subjects connected with their experience the preceding year in connection with these same units and subjects.
3. Scanning text and reference books.
4. Examining courses of study to determine types of words likely to be encountered in carrying out the suggested activities.
5. Rating the words collected from all these various sources as to their probable frequency of encounter by the children, and eliminating the less frequent.
6. Checking all words against the frequencies of occurrence as given in the Thorndike word list.
7. Making the lists from each of the three units equal in number of words by eliminating the necessary number by random selection.
8. Making the list from history and geography equal in number of words to the total of the three lists from the three social studies units.

In collecting words from the teachers it was assumed that their previous experience with the units would give validity to their judgment of the words most likely to be encountered by the children in pursuing the work of the course. They were asked to suggest words which were most frequently used and upon an understanding of which the work of the unit or subjects depended. In order to obtain the words from the various teachers, a letter was sent out in County A by the Assistant Superintendent of Schools to the teachers who were to participate in the experiment. So that no teacher would be overburdened with this work, each was made responsible for suggesting words in connection with a single unit, and the units were assigned to the teachers according to the unit which they were to teach first during the experiment. The letter sent out in County A, the one in which the social studies units were taught, was as follows:

—————————, Maryland.
February 13, 1931

My dear Principal and Teacher:

In connection with the study of spelling ability about which we have written you we are anxious to collect a list of words for each of the three units—Cereal Grains, Domesticated Animals, and Cotton. We are asking that the sixth grade teachers of the schools in Group 1 (see letter of February 3) go over the Cotton Unit outline and jot down a list of the more difficult and uncommon words which the pupils will probably encounter during their study of the unit. These words are of the sort that many teachers pick out for special spelling drill during the teaching of the unit. Group 2 will do the same with the Cereal Grain Unit, Group 3 with the Domesticated Animals Unit.

Each teacher should turn over the list of words to the principal who will send them to the office. These lists should be returned by Tuesday, February 17th.

Very truly yours,

————————————————

Assistant Superintendent

In County B, some of the teachers were asked to suggest words in connection with the geography to be covered during the experimental period, and another group was asked to suggest words in connection with the history which was to be taught during the fifteen weeks. The letter which was sent out was similar to the one sent out in County A.

In County A returns were received from approximately seventy-five per cent of the teachers while in County B lists were turned in by slightly less than fifty per cent. The lists varied in length from twenty to a hundred words. Altogether, several hundred words were suggested for each unit and for the two subjects.

The seventh grade children who had taken the work the preceding year were asked to write compositions involving the same subject matter to be covered during the experiment on the assumption that this would give a valid check upon the words actually acquired by boys and girls as a result of the work done. A sampling of several hundred children was taken in the two counties and they were asked during an English period to write compositions on one of several suggested topics, chosen so as to cover information and understanding in relation to the work upon which the experiment was based. These compositions were scanned by the writer to detect words peculiar to the units and the subjects. A list of these unusual words was compiled and checked against the words suggested by the teachers. There was little difference between the two lists. Each word suggested by one or more teachers was used by two or more pupils. No frequency count was made since this would have involved an amount of labor which could hardly have been justified by the results.

The principal text and reference books and a good share of other reference material used in both counties were scanned in an attempt to determine the more frequently used specialized words. These lists were again compared with the lists resulting from the suggestions of the teachers. This procedure added a number of words to the lists.

The courses of study for the two counties differed considerably in form. In County A, where there was no basic textbook and where wide reference reading was necessary, a considerable amount of basic content material for the teachers appeared in the course of study. In County B the course of study was a mere outline, but it indicated activities and references which were deemed most important. This proved of value in connection with the lists already compiled. In scanning the courses of study a few additional words, particularly in County A, were added to the basic lists.

The rating of the words which had been collected from these various sources according to their probable frequency of encounter by the children was not so difficult as might appear. They were rated subjectively by the writer and this rating was checked by the frequency of the words in general reading as determined by Thorndike. As a result of the scanning of the varied materials, as already described, it was possible to rate each word as "frequent," "less frequent," or "rare," relative to its likelihood of encounter by the children during the experiment, with fair assurance of the reliability of the rating. It would not be expected that the results by this method would coincide with the frequency of the use of the words in general reading materials, for the units and the subjects taught during the experiment represented specialized subject matter. The judgment of teachers and pupils, together with a first-hand scanning of the materials of instruction, would give a rating of probable occurrence in the special materials of the study more appropriate than that afforded by such a list as Thorndike's, in which the words are listed with a designation representing their frequency in general reading.[1] Accordingly, therefore, the words which were rated "rare" were eliminated because, in the judgment of the writer, they occurred too infrequently in the instructional materials. The remaining words were about equally divided between "frequent" and "less frequent."

Next the words were checked against Thorndike's list of the 10,000 commonest words.[2] This was necessary in order to eliminate words which came among the three thousand commonest words in general reading. Under the conditions of the study these words were ruled out. This also afforded a rough means of determining the comparability of the lists for the three experimental groups in County A and the group in County B. The methods and results of this comparison are reported in detail below.

The lists, compiled by the methods just described, varied in length from fifty-five to seventy words for each of the three social studies units and from seventy-five to eighty words in length for history and geography, respectively. It was necessary to make the three lists from the social studies units equal in length, and the list from history and geography equal to the total length of the three unit lists. This was done by eliminating the required number of words by random selection. The completed list for each unit then

[1] Edward L. Thorndike, *The Teacher's Word Book*. Bureau of Publications, Teachers College, Columbia University, New York, 1921.

[2] At the time the test was being prepared Thorndike's longer list had not appeared.

contained fifty words. Because of a number of duplications the total length of the list for the three units was 136 words rather than the 150. The list from history and geography numbered 136 words. It was made up of sixty-eight words from geography and seventy-one words from history. The total of 139 words was reduced to the required 136 by the elimination of three words which appeared in both lists. Thus the conditions of the experiment were met; each child in a "unit group" was examined on a list which included fifty words from the unit which he studied first. At the end of fifteen weeks he was examined on a list made up equally of words from the three units and totaling 136 words out of the 260 in the test. The children in County B likewise were examined by the same test, which included 136 words from the materials of instruction in history and geography which they had studied during the fifteen weeks.[3] So far as length of the lists and sources of the words are concerned, the various groups were examined by an instrument which was equally fair to all.

*Comparability of the Words Making up the Test.* There is no accurate way of determining whether the words making up a particular list are exactly comparable to the words making up the other lists so far as affording a measure of the words incidentally acquired by the children in the work of the unit or subject. That they are approximately comparable seems a reasonable assumption from the fact that identical techniques were used in compiling each of them. A rough approximation of their comparability is afforded, however, by checking the words for frequency in the Thorndike list. This is made possible by using Thorndike's new list which extends the words to 20,000 and by using additional sources for word counts, which gives a better measure of frequency in general reading material for children and young people.[4] Two things should be noted in connection with this comparison, however. One is the evident fact that the commonness or rarity of a word is not a close measure of its difficulty. Undoubtedly there is a positive correlation between frequency of occurrence and the

[3] For explanation of total of 260 instead of 272, see page 28.
[4] Edward L. Thorndike, *Teacher's Word Book of 20,000 Words.* Bureau of Publications, Teachers College, Columbia University, New York, 1931.

ease with which a word may be spelled, but this correlation is probably not high. The other fact is that a measure of frequency in general reading is not a measure of the frequency with which the word will be encountered in the special work of the children in connection with the experiment.

There were 260 words in the final form of the test as indicated above. Each word was checked against the list and a notation made of the "thousand" in which Thorndike had found the word to appear. Thus a notation "4" indicated that the word was not among the first three thousand commonest words, but was included among the four thousand commonest; it fell in the fourth thousand of frequency of occurrence. Ten words did not appear among the 20,000. These words are given in Table I. It is interesting to note that while these words are very rare in the general reading material for children and young people, they are common enough in the subject matter indicated and none is particularly difficult to spell. It should also be noted that five of the words occurred in the history and geography material and five in the material of the social studies.

TABLE I

*Words Which Appear in Special Spelling Test, Not Included Among Thorndike's List of 20,000 Commonest Words, with Unit in Which Word Was Found*

| Word | Unit or Subject |
|------|-----------------|
| beer | Geography |
| chutes | Cereal Grains |
| discus | History |
| Hellespont | History |
| lariat | Domesticated Animals |
| lasso | Domesticated Animals |
| rickshaw | Geography |
| sombrero | Domesticated Animals |
| stylus | History |
| tillable | Cereal Grains |

The three lists of fifty words each, which were compiled from the material of the three social studies units, are given in Tables II, III, and IV. The footnotes in each table indicate the words

## TABLE II

*Words from Cotton Unit Which Appear in Special Spelling Test, and Frequency of Use as Given in Thorndike's List of 20,000 Commonest Words*

| Word | Thousand | Word | Thousand |
|---|---|---|---|
| 1. abolition | 8 | 26. hoe | 4 |
| 2. accommodation | 6 | 27. hosiery | 9 |
| 3. annexation | 11 | 28. husk** | 4 |
| 4. bleach | 6 | 29. importation | 10 |
| 5. bobbin | 18 | 30. impoverish | 10 |
| 6. boll | 18 | 31. institution | 4 |
| 7. calico | 8 | 32. irrigation* | 7 |
| 8. commodity | 7 | 33. latitude* | 7 |
| 9. Confederate | 7 | 34. lint | 12 |
| 10. consumption | 6 | 35. loom | 5 |
| 11. cretonne | 10 | 36. migration*** | 9 |
| 12. culture | 6 | 37. mountaineer | 8 |
| 13. dependency | 10 | 38. oleomargarine*** | 16 |
| 14. distaff | 10 | 39. overseer | 13 |
| 15. diversified | 15 | 40. plantation | 5 |
| 16. drought* | 8 | 41. planter | 6 |
| 17. exclusion | 9 | 42. reconstruction | 9 |
| 18. expansion | 7 | 43. rotation | 7 |
| 19. exploitation** | 17 | 44. secede | 11 |
| 20. export | 5 | 45. slavery | 5 |
| 21. fabric | 6 | 46. spindle | 5 |
| 22. fertilizer* | 6 | 47. spirituals | 4 |
| 23. fiber (re) | 5 | 48. textile | 10 |
| 24. geographical | 8 | 49. transportation | 4 |
| 25. gin | 6 | 50. warp | 5 |

Read table as follows: "*Abolition* is found in the eighth thousand; *annexation* in the eleventh thousand, etc.*"

* Included also in lists from the cereal grains and domesticated animals units.
** Included also in list for cereal grains unit.
*** Included also in list for domesticated animals unit.

duplicated in the lists. This brings the total of the three when combined to 136 different words. With each word is given the "thousand" in which it appears in Thorndike's list of 20,000 words. Similarly, the list of sixty-eight words taken from the geography material is given in Table V and the seventy-one words from the history material in Table VI. Duplicated words are again indicated by footnotes.

A frequency distribution was made of the Thorndike ratings

## TABLE III

*Words from Cereal Grain Unit Which Appear in Special Spelling Test, and Frequency of Use as Given in Thorndike's List of 20,000 Commonest Words*

| Word | Thousand | Word | Thousand |
|---|---|---|---|
| 1. alluvial | 12 | 26. husk** | 6 |
| 2. barley | 4 | 27. intensive | 16 |
| 3. bran | 6 | 28. irrigation* | 7 |
| 4. chaff | 5 | 29. jute | 11 |
| 5. chutes[1] | — | 30. latitude* | 7 |
| 6. civilization | 7 | 31. loam | 11 |
| 7. competition | 6 | 32. millet | 11 |
| 8. consumer | 9 | 33. monotonous | 8 |
| 9. cyclonic | 20 | 34. monsoon | 18 |
| 10. delta | 6 | 35. nourishment | 6 |
| 11. drought* | 8 | 36. Oriental | 6 |
| 12. elevator | 7 | 37. prairie*** | 5 |
| 13. embryo | 7 | 38. primitive | 7 |
| 14. equatorial | 10 | 39. protein | 7 |
| 15. Euphrates | 9 | 40. resources | 6 |
| 16. exploitation** | 17 | 41. rye | 4 |
| 17. facilities*** | 7 | 42. sheaves | 7 |
| 18. fermentation | 8 | 43. sieve | 6 |
| 19. fertilizer* | 6 | 44. stagnant | 7 |
| 20. fodder | 6 | 45. terrace | 6 |
| 21. germinate | 9 | 46. thresher | 17 |
| 22. granary | 11 | 47. tillable[1] | — |
| 23. gum | 5 | 48. transplant | 10 |
| 24. harrow | 6 | 49. vitamin (e) | 11 |
| 25. healthful | 6 | 50. volcano | 7 |

Read table as follows: "*Alluvial* is found in the twelfth thousand; *barley* in the fourth thousand, etc."

[1] Not listed among the 20,000 words in Thorndike's list.
* Included also in list for domesticated animals and cotton units.
** Included also in cotton unit.
*** Included also in domesticated animals unit.

for the words in each list, and for the combined social studies list and the combined history and geography list. The results are shown in Table VII. The median rating of the three social studies lists varied by less than one step (a "step" representing a "thousand" as used by Thorndike) from the rating of 8.85 for the Domesticated Animals Unit to the rating of 7.91 for the Cotton Unit. The actual difference was .94 of a step. The inter-quartile ranges of the three lists varied to a greater degree, however. The

### TABLE IV

*Words from Domesticated Animals Unit Which Appear in Special Spelling Test, and Frequency of Use as Given in Thorndike's List of 20,000 Commonest Words*

| Word | Thousand | Word | Thousand |
|------|----------|------|----------|
| 1. adapted | 8 | 26. incubator | 11 |
| 2. adulterated | 12 | 27. insoluble | 9 |
| 3. alfalfa | 7 | 28. intestine | 9 |
| 4. ancestor | 16 | 29. irrigation* | 7 |
| 5. broncho | 17 | 30. lariat[1] | — |
| 6. browse | 11 | 31. lasso[1] | — |
| 7. calves | 6 | 32. latitude* | 7 |
| 8. carcass | 8 | 33. migration*** | 9 |
| 9. certified | 10 | 34. mountainous | 5 |
| 10. characteristics | 5 | 35. mutton | 5 |
| 11. condensed | 6 | 36. oleomargarine*** | 16 |
| 12. corral | 14 | 37. originate | 8 |
| 13. coyote | 13 | 38. pasteurize | 14 |
| 14. creamery | 10 | 39. plateau | 5 |
| 15. descendants | 7 | 40. pommel | 14 |
| 16. disinfectant | 13 | 41. prairie** | 5 |
| 17. drought* | 8 | 42. refrigerator | 9 |
| 18. evaporated | 8 | 43. sausage | 5 |
| 19. ewe | 4 | 44. scythe | 8 |
| 20. exposure | 8 | 45. silo | 18 |
| 21. facilities** | 7 | 46. slaughter | 4 |
| 22. fertilizer* | 6 | 47. sombrero[1] | — |
| 23. fleece | 4 | 48. stampede | 14 |
| 24. forage | 8 | 49. sterile | 10 |
| 25. Guernsey | 13 | 50. tuberculin | 18 |

Read table as follows: "*Adapted* is found in the eighth thousand; *adulterated* in the twelfth thousand, etc."

[1] Not listed among the 20,000 words in Thorndike's list.
* Included also in lists for the cereal grains and cotton units.
** Included also in cereal grains unit.
*** Included also in cotton unit.

Cotton Unit list had the least range, 4.30, while the Domesticated Animals Unit list had the greatest range, it being 6.54. It is safe to conclude that three lists are similar in the type of words represented, so far as the Thorndike rating indicates, but that the lists differ in the range of words which are used.

The ratings of the words from history and from geography are also given, merely to indicate their similarity. It is not necessary

## TABLE V

*Words from Geography Materials Which Appear in Special Spelling Test, and Frequency of Use as Given in Thorndike's List of 20,000 Commonest Words*

| Word | Thousand | Word | Thousand |
|---|---|---|---|
| 1. alcohol | 7 | 35. Mongolian | 14 |
| 2. arctic | 5 | 36. monsoon | 18 |
| 3. barge | 6 | 37. mountainous* | 5 |
| 4. beer¹ | — | 38. mulberry | 7 |
| 5. Belgium | 6 | 39. navigable | 6 |
| 6. brewery | 14 | 40. Netherlands | 5 |
| 7. camel | 4 | 41. nitrogen | 7 |
| 8. chemical | 8 | 42. nomad | 9 |
| 9. cocoon | 10 | 43. ore | 10 |
| 10. creamery | 10 | 44. Oriental | 6 |
| 11. currants | 6 | 45. peat | 19 |
| 12. dikes | 12 | 46. peninsula | 5 |
| 13. earthquake | 4 | 47. petroleum | 6 |
| 14. educated | 6 | 48. plateau | 5 |
| 15. electricity | 7 | 49. Portugal | 6 |
| 16. embroidery | 5 | 50. potash | 12 |
| 17. estuaries | 13 | 51. pottery* | 11 |
| 18. extensive | 5 | 52. prosperity | 4 |
| 19. fertilizer | 6 | 53. refinery | 10 |
| 20. fiord | 13 | 54. Rhine | 5 |
| 21. flax | 4 | 55. rickshaw¹ | — |
| 22. galleries | 4 | 56. rotate | 9 |
| 23. glacial | 15 | 57. Scandinavia | 10 |
| 24. horticulture | 20 | 58. scenery | 7 |
| 25. illuminate | 7 | 59. seaport | 6 |
| 26. intensive | 16 | 60. smelting | 6 |
| 27. international | 8 | 61. textile | 10 |
| 28. irrigation | 7 | 62. thatch | 8 |
| 29. kimono | 12 | 63. transportation | 4 |
| 30. lignite | 15 | 64. tributary | 4 |
| 31. location | 4 | 65. tulips | 9 |
| 32. lumberman | 12 | 66. vineyard* | 6 |
| 33. mackerel | 11 | 67. volcano | 7 |
| 34. mineral | 4 | 68. wharves | 7 |

Read table as follows: *"Alcohol is found in the seventh thousand; arctic, in the fifth thousand, etc."*

¹ Not listed among the 20,000 words.
* Included also in list from history materials.

## TABLE VI

*Words from History Materials Which Appear in Special Spelling Test, and Frequency of Use as Given in Thorndike's List of 20,000 Commonest Words*

| Word | Thousand | Word | Thousand |
|------|----------|------|----------|
| 1. acropolis | 19 | 36. Hellespont[1] | — |
| 2. amphitheatre | 14 | 37. herdsman | 8 |
| 3. aqueduct | 12 | 38. invader | 8 |
| 4. architect | 7 | 39. Jesuit | 12 |
| 5. barbarian | 7 | 40. literature | 4 |
| 6. basilica | 19 | 41. manuscript | 7 |
| 7. Caesar | 3 | 42. mariner | 5 |
| 8. caravan | 6 | 43. massacre | .8 |
| 9. cathedral | 4 | 44. moat | 8 |
| 10. catholic | 4 | 45. monastery | 9 |
| 11. cinnamon | 10 | 46. mosaic | 9 |
| 12. circumnavigate | 13 | 47. mosque | 14 |
| 13. citadel | 10 | 48. mountainous* | 5 |
| 14. civilization | 7 | 49. navigation | 7 |
| 15. code | 8 | 50. Olympic | 17 |
| 16. colonist | 4 | 51. papyrus | 17 |
| 17. conqueror | 4 | 52. Parthenon | 14 |
| 18. continuation | 8 | 53. patrician | 14 |
| 19. costume | 5 | 54. persecution | 6 |
| 20. craftsman | 10 | 55. pilgrim | 4 |
| 21. crusade | 8 | 56. plebeian | 8 |
| 22. discipline | 5 | 57. Portuguese | 6 |
| 23. discus[1] | — | 58. pottery* | 11 |
| 24. drawbridge | 13 | 59. precipice | 7 |
| 25. emigrant | 9 | 60. protestant | 7 |
| 26. explorer | 7 | 61. Raleigh | 8 |
| 27. festival | 4 | 62. renaissance | 11 |
| 28. feudalism | 18 | 63. Saxon | 8 |
| 29. forum | 10 | 64. sculpture | 7 |
| 30. friars | 5 | 65. sickle | 6 |
| 31. frieze | 9 | 66. Socrates | 10 |
| 32. frontier | 6 | 67. Sparta | 9 |
| 33. goldsmith | 8 | 68. stadium | 16 |
| 34. gladiator | 11 | 69. stylus[1] | — |
| 35. gunpowder | 6 | 70. tunic | 10 |
| | | 71. vineyard* | 6 |

Read table as follows "*Acropolis* is found in the nineteenth thousand; *amphitheatre*, in the fourteenth thousand, etc."

[1] Not listed among the 20,000 words.
* Included also in list from geography materials.

## TABLE VII

*Medians, Quartiles, and Inter-Quartile Ranges of Ratings of Words Composing*
*Special Spelling Test as Given in Thorndike's List of 20,000 Commonest Words*

| Source of Words | Cotton Unit | Cereal Grains Unit | Domesticated Animals Unit | Social Studies Units | History | Geography | History and Geography |
|---|---|---|---|---|---|---|---|
| Upper Quartile | 10.30 | 11.17 | 13.43 | 11.50 | 11.90 | 11.33 | 11.60 |
| Median ....... | 7.91 | 8.07 | 8.85 | 8.38 | 8.55 | 7.83 | 8.31 |
| Lower Quartile | 6.00 | 6.40 | 6.89 | 6.33 | 6.63 | 5.80 | 6.13 |
| Inter-Quartile Range ..... | 4.30 | 4.77 | 6.54 | 5.17 | 5.27 | 5.53 | 5.47 |
| Number of Words ..... | 50 | 50 | 50 | 136 | 71 | 68 | 136 |

that they be precisely equal since comparisons are made on the basis of the combined list from the two sources.

But the comparability of the total list from social studies and the total list from history and geography is significant, and it is noteworthy that the two show almost identical median ratings and have very similar inter-quartile ranges. Thus the difference between the median rating of the social studies list, 8.38, and the history and geography list, 8.31, is only .07. The difference between the inter-quartile range of 5.47 for the history and geography list and 5.17 for the social studies list is slightly larger, though it amounts to only .30. So far, then, as the Thorndike ratings are a measure of difficulty or probability of encounter, the two lists may be said to be equal.

*Assembling the Test.* The procedure of selecting the words has been described and an indication given of the comparability of the words for the several situations. But it was necessary to combine the lists into one master list which would constitute the test. There were 136 words from the social studies units, and 136 words from the history and geography material. In combining these groups twelve words were found to be included in both. These twelve words are shown in Table VIII. The test, then, consisted of 260 different words.

In order to give an equal opportunity to the students in each of

### TABLE VIII

*Twelve Words Which Appear in Both Combined Social Studies
List and Combined History and Geography List*

| | | |
|---|---|---|
| civilization | irrigation | plateau |
| creamery | monsoon | textile |
| fertilizer | mountainous | transportation |
| intensive | Oriental | volcano |

the groups the words were arranged in such order that out of each twenty-four words, twelve were from history and geography and twelve from social studies, the latter being made up of four words from each of the three units. This was the general system followed, although duplicated words caused slight discrepancies. The words were in approximate alphabetical order but the procedure followed caused the final list to vary greatly from an actual alphabetical arrangement.

The choice of testing methods offered a real problem. Research findings on this point are inconclusive. Guiler,[5] for example, compared three testing methods, oral recall, written recall, and multiple choice, to discover which had the greatest validity. The oral recall method is described as consisting of pronunciation of the word, and its use in a meaningful sentence by the examiner, followed by each pupil's writing the word on a prepared blank piece of paper. In the written recall method a prepared test paper was used in which each word, in its most frequently misspelled form, appeared within parentheses as a regular part of a meaningful sentence, the pupil being required to write the correct spelling within the blank parentheses at the end of the line. The multiple choice method used a test paper on which were four spellings of each test word within parentheses as a part of a meaningful sentence, the pupil being required to underline the correct spelling. The criterion used in this study "for establishing the validity of methods of testing spelling is the potency with which the different methods discover words that pupils cannot spell."[6] The basic assumption here, of course, is that pupils either do or do not know how to spell a word; there is no halfway point. Apparently if a

[5] Walter S. Guiler, "Validation of Methods of Testing Spelling." *Journal of Educational Research*, XX (October, 1929), pp. 181-189.

[6] Guiler, *op. cit.*, p. 181.

pupil knows how to spell a word he can spell it under any conditions, orally, in writing, in a testing, or what not. Even the recognition of correctly and incorrectly spelled words is assumed to be the same thing as spelling it when the word is needed in writing. That method was held to be most valid in which the pupils, on the average, misspelled the most words. That this was a valid criterion is seriously open to question. Actually only a part of the time does one have need of the ability to recognize misspellings, for this skill is used only in revising one's own written work or in proofreading. The great bulk of the writing of the average individual is left in its original form. Presenting misspellings to pupils is probably bad from the psychological point of view as tending to "fix" the wrong response. The criterion of validity must go back to the definition of spelling ability. Upon this point there is considerable disagreement. It seems reasonable to hold that the spelling ability with which the schools should be concerned is the ability of the child to spell the words he needs to use in his written expression. If this is accepted, then the only true criterion of validity will be a measure based upon an analysis of the child's written expression. It will not only include how correctly he spells the words he actually uses, but it will also take into account the level of difficulty of these words. Only thus will due allowance be made for the child who spells correctly, using only the simplest words, or the child who consciously avoids words as too difficult to spell that he might otherwise use. Such a measure may be costly to obtain and impractical for general use. It will serve, however, as a criterion against which "short-cut" methods may be validated.

Using the criterion of the greatest number of misspellings, Guiler concluded that the written recall method was on the whole the most effective testing technique. In another experiment, however, in which only the oral recall and the written recall were compared, the oral recall test was found to be superior. The study is obviously inconclusive.

A comparison of testing methods using an even more doubtful technique is given in a study reported by T. G. Foran.[7] The investi-

[7] T. G. Foran, *The Form of Spelling Tests,* Educational Research Bulletins, The Catholic University of America, Vol. IV, No. 8 (October, 1929). The Catholic Education Press, Washington, D. C.

gator used lists of words from the Morrison-McCall Spelling Scale and constructed six different types of tests. Major reliance is placed upon computed intercorrelations as a measure of validity, though relative difficulty is also mentioned. No actual criterion of validity is given. Three of the tests were tried with 215 pupils in grades three, four, and five. The intercorrelations were all above .800. With the reliability coefficient of the test reported as .893 Foran concludes that "the figures seem to indicate that the correlations between these three forms of spelling tests approach very closely to the reliability coefficients and that they are as high as possible."[8] This would seem to indicate that all three methods gave very similar results. But since no standard of validity is given, it cannot be concluded whether they are equally good or equally bad. Difficulty is mentioned in passing by noting that "if Guiler's criterion be employed, the sentence form is best, as it discovers more misspellings."[9]

In the second part of the investigation six types of testing were used with 207 pupils in grades six, seven, and eight. Means, standard deviations, and intercorrelations were computed. Conclusions are given regarding the relative difficulty of the various methods of testing spelling which seem to be warranted by the data. But Foran also concludes that the "correlations show that the form of the test is an important factor in the measurement of spelling. So far as the data answer the question at issue, they indicate that recognition tests are unsatisfactory and that the results therefrom cannot be compared with those from recall tests."[10] But since no criterion of validity has been stated such a conclusion seems unwarranted. It is perfectly possible, for example, that a test method which might correlate most highly with the actual ability of students to spell the words needed in written expression might correlate much less with other types of tests because the latter were all poor measures of spelling ability. So far as the experimental data presented in this report are concerned, they fail to clarify the problem of method of testing. The final sentence in the study, which is

---

[8] *Ibid.,* p. 16.
[9] *Ibid.,* p. 16.
[10] *Ibid.,* p. 21.

based more upon observation than research, is probably the most helpful in the entire pamphlet. Concludes the author:

> . . . On the basis of facility of administration, time, and freedom from ambiguities of meaning and pronunciation, the modified sentence type of test seems as satisfactory as any other and superior to most forms.[11]

Another comparison of testing methods is that which was made by Pintner, Rinsland, and Zubin.[12] They frankly state that the criterion, the Morrison-McCall Spelling Scale, was selected because this test was reported by Kelley to have been given a rating of "one" by five judges. Other types of testing were therefore correlated with this test as a criterion. The inadequacy of using such a criterion merely because it is rated by judges as being the "best" test is evident. The conclusions which the authors drew are that the two experimental forms of self-administering tests in spelling were valid and reliable as group spelling tests because they correlated highly with the criterion. Since the criterion, the Morrison-McCall Spelling Scale, uses the modified sentence form, it would not be possible to determine by this means whether any of the experimental forms were better measures of spelling ability than the criterion.

The most complete recent study of spelling methods is that by Cook.[13] While he defines validity in the usual way as the degree to which a test measures what it is intended to measure, he uses as the criterion for correlating various types of tests the scores obtained on a 150-word test given by the modified sentence technique, the words being taken from the ten thousand in Horn's *A Basic Writing Vocabulary*. His basic assumption, therefore, is that the results on this test are a true measure of spelling ability. No experimental evidence is presented as a basis for this assumption. It is apparent from his discussion of testing techniques that Cook confuses the validity of subject matter with the validity of a

---

[11] *Ibid.*, p. 24.

[12] R. Pintner, H. D. Rinsland, and J. Zubin, "The Evaluation of Self-Administering Spelling Tests." *Journal of Educational Psychology*, XX (February, 1929), pp. 107-111.

[13] Walter Wellman Cook, *The Measurement of General Spelling Ability Involving Controlled Comparisons Between Techniques.* University of Iowa, Studies in Education, Vol. VI, No. 6. The University, Iowa City, February 15, 1932.

test for measuring an ability. Thus he infers that since Horn's list is generally accepted as a basic spelling vocabulary, a long and very reliable test based upon this list must necessarily be valid. This is true only (1) if it be granted that spelling ability consists of the ability to spell these common words, and (2) if the modified sentence technique (which he used) is accepted as the most valid technique for measuring this ability.

Accepting the scores of the pupils on the 150-word test as the criterion of validity, Cook compares various testing techniques, draws conclusions regarding the selection of test items, the optimum time of administration, and the spelling ability of boys and girls. The obvious conclusion regarding the choice of a technique for testing on a larger number of words is that the modified sentence technique has not been shown to be inferior since it is accepted as a criterion.

As a result of this survey of the investigations comparing different methods of testing spelling ability it is clear that the modified sentence technique in which the word is pronounced, used in an illustrative sentence, and pronounced again, after which it is written by the pupil, has not been shown to be invalid. The investigators either accept it as a valid criterion, or, as in the case of Guiler, use a criterion of validity which is questionable. Until an extensive investigation is made based upon such a valid criterion as has been suggested, the modified sentence technique will probably continue to be accepted as a satisfactory method of testing spelling. It is the one which was adopted for the present study.

The preparing of illustrative sentences was a comparatively simple task. The writer attempted to use simple words, other than the words being tested, and to make the sentences as typical of the subject matter of the unit or subject from which the word was derived as possible. Since the pupils needed to write only the test words and not the entire sentence, it was only necessary that the sentences be made up of words, in addition to the test words, which the pupils would understand.

Instructions for administering the test were prepared which would make the conditions under which the test was given as uniform as possible. In order to avoid fatigue the test was divided into four sittings of sixty-five words each. While fifty words is usually considered the optimum number of words to be given at a sitting, it was believed that sixth grade children would be able to extend this number to sixty-five without undue fatigue' which might affect the results, particularly since many of the words were unfamiliar to them.

The instructions were mimeographed and accompanied the mimeographed copies of the word list. These were sent out to the schools each time the test was to be administered and were collected, together with the test papers, immediately after the giving of the test. This precaution was taken in order to avoid the possibility of teachers attempting to teach the words to the children. The list was so long, 260 words, that it was believed practically impossible for either teachers or children to remember many of the words upon which the pupils were tested.

*Final Form of the Test.* The test, in its final form, and the instructions for administering it are given below:

INSTRUCTIONS FOR GIVING THE TEST

The following instructions are to be observed when giving the test:

The test is to be given in four sittings, with 65 words to a sitting. The pupils should use blank sheets of paper for each sitting. At the top of the sheet have the pupils write their names and the name of the school and teacher. They should be able to get three columns on the page, each column containing 22 words (except the last which, of course, will have 21 words). One sitting should be given in the morning and one in the afternoon. The test will take two days.

Teachers will give the test but the papers will be scored by clerks and will not require the attention of the teachers.

After the tests have been given the papers should be returned to the office of the principal, together with the list of words and these instructions. The principal will return this material to the Board of Education Office.

In reading the words for the pupils, first pronounce the word, then read the illustrative sentence, and then pronounce the word again. The word or the illustrative sentence may be repeated if necessary but no other explanation of the word other than the illustrative sentence should be given. The pupils, of course, will merely write the word, not the illustrative sentence.

Be sure to give the number of the word before pronouncing each new word so that pupils may not get mixed up. The pupils should number the words so that they will not omit a word. Thus, in reading say: "Number 114. (pause) *granary* (pause) The wheat was placed in the granary. (pause) *granary.*"

After seeing that pupils have blank sheets of paper and pencils, have them write their names at the top of the page. Underneath this they should write the name of the school and the name of the teacher. Then say:

"We are going to have a spelling test. The words which you are to be tested on are not easy words. Some of them are very hard words, and some of them you may not have heard of before. So do not be disappointed if you cannot spell many of them. However, you should all do the best that you can with these words, for we want to see how well you can spell hard words. There will be 65 words, so you will want to get 22 words in each column except the last, and have three columns on the page. Number from 1 to 22 on the left hand side of the page and then we will begin the test. (See that this is done.) Listen very carefully while I read the instructions. I will first give you the number of the word and then read the word to you. Then I will use the word in a sentence so that you will know exactly what word is meant. Then I will pronounce the word again. Be sure you know what word is meant, if the word is not new to you, and then write it the best way you can. Do your best but do not worry about words you cannot spell. Ready! Number one. (pause) *abolition*—etc."

For the second sitting, say: "Now we are going to have another spelling test just like the one we had this morning. Be sure to write your name, and the name of the school and my name at the top of the page just as you did before. Begin numbering down the left hand side of the page with number 66 and number to 87." Proceed as before.

The third and fourth sittings will be exactly the same except for the numbering which will begin in one case with 131 and in the other with 196.

It would be well to look over the words and be sure you are familiar with the pronunciation of all of them. Look up doubtful ones such as *renaissance*, etc.

## SPECIAL SPELLING TEST

| Word | Illustrative Sentence |
|---|---|
| 1. abolition | He worked for the abolition of slavery. |
| 2. annexation | He did not like the annexation of Texas by the United States. |
| 3. alluvial | The city was located on an alluvial plain. |
| 4. ancestor | Her ancestor had been a duke. |
| 5. alcohol | He put alcohol into the radiator. |
| 6. arctic | It is cold in the arctic regions. |
| 7. Acropolis | The Acropolis is now in ruins. |
| 8. amphitheater (re) | The amphitheater was crowded with people. |
| 9. accommodations | They found accommodations at the hotel. |
| 10. aqueduct | The aqueduct brought water for 75 miles. |
| 11. barley | Barley is raised in Russia. |

## SPECIAL SPELLING TEST (*Continued*)

| *Word* | *Illustrative Sentence* |
|---|---|
| 12. architect | The architect planned a new postoffice. |
| 13. bleach | They will bleach the cotton before selling it. |
| 14. beer | Beer is the national drink of Germany. |
| 15. alfalfa | Alfalfa makes good hay. |
| 16. brewery | The brewery was the largest in Germany. |
| 17. bran | Bran muffins are healthful. |
| 18. barge | The barge was loaded with lumber. |
| 19. adapted | It was years before they became adapted to the cold weather. |
| 20. Belgium | Belgium is not a large country. |
| 21. bobbin | The bobbin in the spinning machine was broken. |
| 22. barbarian | He was a barbarian from the North. |
| 23. chutes | The bundles were thrown into chutes which led to the trucks. |
| 24. basilica | The basilica was an interesting building. |
| 25. adulterated | The food had been adulterated. |
| 26. chemical | The bottle contained a brown chemical. |
| 27. boll | The cotton boll is full of seeds. |
| 28. currants | They spent the morning picking currants. |
| 29. cyclonic | Cyclonic storms cause many of our changes of weather. |
| 30. cocoon | Silk is made from the cocoon of a silk-worm. |
| 31. browse | The cattle like to browse on the hillsides. |
| 32. camel | He rode a camel across the desert. |
| 33. calico | She wore a calico dress. |
| 34. citadel | The army defended the citadel. |
| 35. consumer | When rice reaches the consumer the husks have been removed. |
| 36. code | The message was written in code so that the enemy could not read it. |
| 37. broncho | He rode a broncho on the ranch. |
| 38. Caesar | Caesar was the Emperor of Rome. |
| 39. cretonne | The curtains were made of cretonne. |
| 40. conqueror | He was finally conqueror of three nations. |
| 41. chaff | The chaff from wheat is not good to eat. |
| 42. circumnavigate | Today you can circumnavigate the globe in a month. |
| 43. creamery | The creamery sold butter to merchants in New York. |
| 44. cathedral | The cathedral was large and very beautiful. |
| 45. Confederate | He belonged to the Confederate army. |
| 46. crusades | The crusades made a change in the life of the Middle Ages. |
| 47. civilization | The Indians did not have much civilization. |
| 48. caravan | It took the caravan three weeks to cross the desert. |
| 49. condensed | She put condensed milk in her coffee. |
| 50. colonists | The colonists who settled New England were very religious. |

## SPECIAL SPELLING TEST (*Continued*)

| *Word* | *Illustrative Sentence* |
|---|---|
| 51. commodity | Tea is a commodity which we buy from other countries. |
| 52. craftsman | The craftsman carved a beautiful toy dog. |
| 53. competition | There is a great deal of competition between the two schools. |
| 54. costume | Her costume made her look like a witch. |
| 55. corral | The horse was put into the corral. |
| 56. Catholic | The Catholic church is the oldest of Christian churches. |
| 57. consumption | There is a large consumption of rice among the Chinese. |
| 58. continuation | The Second Crusade was a sort of continuation of the first. |
| 59. delta | A large delta is located at the mouth of the river. |
| 60. cinnamon | Cinnamon is a spice. |
| 61. characteristics | What are the characteristics of the American people? |
| 62. dikes | Dikes have been built in Holland to keep the water off the land. |
| 63. dependency | Hawaii is a dependency of the United States. |
| 64. discus | He threw the discus a great distance. |
| 65. elevator | There was plenty of wheat in the elevator. |
| 66. discipline | Sparta was noted for its strict discipline. |
| 67. carcass | The carcass of a horse lay stretched out in the desert. |
| 68. drawbridge | A drawbridge spans the Harlem river in New York. |
| 69. drought | The South has been suffering with a drought. |
| 70. electricity | Electricity is often made from water power. |
| 71. equatorial | The equatorial regions are very hot. |
| 72. estuaries | The river divided into several estuaries. |
| 73. certified | She fed the baby certified milk. |
| 74. educated | He was well educated. |
| 75. distaff | The distaff was broken and she could not go on with her spinning. |
| 76. earthquake | Earthquakes are common in California. |
| 77. Euphrates | The Euphrates is a large river. |
| 78. extensive | Extensive farming is carried on in Kansas. |
| 79. calves | Seven calves were born on the farm that year. |
| 80. embroidery | She made some pretty embroidery. |
| 81. diversified | The Swiss have diversified occupations. |
| 82. explorer | He was a famous explorer of Africa. |
| 83. embryo | A seed is a whole plant in embryo. |
| 84. emigrant | She was an emigrant from Russia. |
| 85. coyote | The coyote howled for half the night. |
| 86. flax | Linen is made from flax. |
| 87. exclusion | The exclusion of the Japanese from America caused hard feelings. |
| 88. fiord | The Norwegian fiord extended several miles inland. |

## SPECIAL SPELLING TEST (*Continued*)

| *Word* | *Illustrative Sentence* |
|---|---|
| 89. fodder | The cows were fed on fodder. |
| 90. festival | A great festival was held in the streets. |
| 91. descendants | The Pilgrims have many descendants. |
| 92. frieze | A frieze showing the progress of the pioneers extended all the way around the room. |
| 93. export | United States will export many cars this year. |
| 94. forum | They held a public forum to discuss the question. |
| 95. facilities | What facilities for athletic games does your school offer? |
| 96. feudalism | Feudalism extended all over Europe in the Middle Ages. |
| 97. disinfectant | A strong disinfectant was used to kill the germs. |
| 98. friar | The friar was very religious. |
| 99. expansion | There was a rapid expansion of trade with Japan. |
| 100. frontier | The frontier kept moving westward. |
| 101. fermentation | Strong drinks are made from the fermentation of grains. |
| 102. glacial | The cut in the rock was due to glacial action. |
| 103. evaporated | Evaporated milk is sold in cans. |
| 104. galleries | The people sat in the galleries. |
| 105. exploitation | There was a great deal of exploitation of the resources of the country. |
| 106. gladiator | A strong gladiator fought with the lion. |
| 107. gum | Gum is used most widely in America. |
| 108. gunpowder | Gunpowder was first used by the Chinese. |
| 109. ewe | The ewe was a cute little animal. |
| 110. goldsmith | The goldsmith worked nearly a year making the crown. |
| 111. fiber (re) | The cotton fiber is made into thread. |
| 112. horticulture | Horticulture is an industry in Holland. |
| 113. germinate | The seed will not germinate for several days. |
| 114. herdsman | A herdsman brought in the cattle. |
| 115. exposure | Too long exposure to the rays of the sun is dangerous in the tropics. |
| 116. Hellespont | He crossed the Hellespont. |
| 117. fertilizer | Putting fertilizer on the field helped the wheat to grow. |
| 118. illuminate | The light will illuminate the room. |
| 119. granary | The wheat was placed in the granary. |
| 120. international | Trade is international these days. |
| 121. forage | The horses were turned loose to forage for food. |
| 122. invader | The invader stole through the wall of the city late at night. |
| 123. fabric | Silk can be made into a fine fabric. |
| 124. Jesuit | The priest was a Jesuit. |
| 125. harrow | It was necessary to harrow the field. |

SPECIAL SPELLING TEST (*Continued*)

| *Word* | *Illustrative Sentence* |
|---|---|
| 126. kimono | She wore a pink kimono. |
| 127. fleece | Wool comes from the fleece of sheep. |
| 128. lignite | Lignite is a low grade of coal. |
| 129. gin | The cotton gin saved the South from much labor. |
| 130. location | What is the location of your school? |
| 131. healthful | Milk is a very healthful drink. |
| 132. lumberman | He was a lumberman from Seattle. |
| 133. Guernsey | The cow was a Guernsey. |
| 134. literature | They studied literature for three years. |
| 135. geographical | What is the geographical location of Maryland? |
| 136. mackerel | He had mackerel for dinner last Friday. |
| 137. intensive | The Chinese do intensive farming. |
| 138. minerals | Gold and silver are important minerals. |
| 139. incubator | The chickens were raised in an incubator. |
| 140. Mongolian | The Mongolian race have yellow skins. |
| 141. insoluble | Coal is insoluble in water. |
| 142. mulberry | Silk worms feed on mulberry leaves. |
| 143. hosiery | Silk hosiery is taking the place of cotton. |
| 144. mosaic | A beautiful mosaic can be seen at the Library of Congress. |
| 145. jute | The jute plant is used for making twine. |
| 146. monastery | The monk lived in a monastery. |
| 147. intestine | Sausage is wrapped in the intestine of the hog. |
| 148. moat | A deep moat surrounded the castle. |
| 149. lariat | He threw the lariat over the horns of the bull. |
| 150. manuscript | He read an old manuscript. |
| 151. hoe | He took the hoe into the garden. |
| 152. mosque | It was a Mohammedan mosque. |
| 153. loam | The soil was a rich loam. |
| 154. lasso | He swung the lasso around his head before throwing it. |
| 155. mariner | The mariner stood at the wheel of the ship. |
| 156. husk | Rice has a husk until it is polished. |
| 157. massacre | The Indian massacre was horrible. |
| 158. monsoons | The monsoons bring heavy rains. |
| 159. nitrogen | Nitrogen is one the gases found in the air. |
| 160. irrigation | Irrigation has changed California into a rich farming state. |
| 161. navigable | The river was navigable only for a short distance. |
| 162. millet | Millet is a grain which is not common in America. |
| 163. Netherlands | The Netherlands is located in Europe. |
| 164. mountainous | Colorado is very mountainous. |
| 165. institution | Our school is a fine institution. |
| 166. nomad | He was a wandering nomad. |
| 167. monotonous | Factory work is sometimes very monotonous. |

## SPECIAL SPELLING TEST (*Continued*)

| Word | Illustrative Sentence |
|---|---|
| 168. navigation | Navigation has stopped on the canal from Washington to Cumberland. |
| 169. mutton | Mutton is eaten in Great Britain. |
| 170. ore | He found a piece of iron ore. |
| 171. importation | They depend upon the importation of wheat from Siberia. |
| 172. Olympic | The Olympic games were great events. |
| 173. nourishment | Rice furnishes nourishment for millions of people. |
| 174. peat | Peat is dug in Ireland. |
| 175. originates | Burbank originates new plants. |
| 176. potash | Potash can be used for fertilizer. |
| 177. Oriental | It was a large Oriental temple. |
| 178. prosperity | The country showed signs of prosperity. |
| 179. impoverish | Too heavy taxes may impoverish the people. |
| 180. peninsula | Italy is located on a peninsula. |
| 181. primitive | The Indians were primitive people. |
| 182. petroleum | Petroleum is found in Oklahoma. |
| 183. prairie | He lived out on the prairie. |
| 184. plateau | The city was located on a high plateau. |
| 185. lint | The floor had not been swept and was covered with lint. |
| 186. Portugal | Portugal is a European country. |
| 187. protein | Beans contain a great deal of protein. |
| 188. Alps | Switzerland is in the Alps mountains. |
| 189. pasteurize | Does Henry know how to pasteurize milk? |
| 190. pottery | He collected old pottery. |
| 191. latitude | In what latitude is Maryland located? |
| 192. Parthenon | The Parthenon is a splendid example of fine architecture. |
| 193. resources | What are the natural resources of the United States? |
| 194. papyrus | The old scrolls were made of papyrus. |
| 195. loom | He worked all day at the cotton loom. |
| 196. patrician | The Roman patrician was considered a gentleman. |
| 197. migration | The migration of the Europeans to America kept growing larger. |
| 198. plebeian | He was a plebeian and had few privileges. |
| 199. mountaineer | The mountaineer lived in the Alps. |
| 200. precipice | Don't fall over the precipice! |
| 201. oleomargarine | Oleomargarine is a substitute for butter. |
| 202. persecution | The persecution of the Christians was terrible. |
| 203. overseer | The overseer had charge of the plantation. |
| 204. pilgrim | The pilgrim started his journey. |
| 205. plantation | It was a large cotton plantation. |
| 206. Protestants | The Protestants objected to some things that the church was doing. |
| 207. planter | The rich planter bought another farm. |

SPECIAL SPELLING TEST (*Continued*)

| *Word* | *Illustrative Sentence* |
|---|---|
| 208. Portuguese | The Portuguese were interested in exploration. |
| 209. rotation | Rotation of crops is often worth while. |
| 210. rye | Rye is a grain resembling wheat. |
| 211. rotate | See the flywheel rotate. |
| 212. reconstruction | The South began the hard work of reconstruction. |
| 213. pommel | He hung onto the pommel of the saddle for fear he would fall. |
| 214. refinery | The crude oil was then taken to the refinery. |
| 215. slavery | Slavery was introduced into the United States in 1610. |
| 216. Rhine | The Rhine is a most important river. |
| 217. sheaves | The sheaves of grain stood in the field. |
| 218. rickshaw | The Chinese merchant rode in a rickshaw. |
| 219. refrigerator | The meat market had a large refrigerator. |
| 220. Raleigh | Sir Walter Raleigh spread his cloak on the ground. |
| 221. secede | The South decided to secede. |
| 222. renaissance | The renaissance brought back the knowledge which had been forgotten. |
| 223. spirituals | The Negroes sang their spirituals beautifully. |
| 224. seaport | Baltimore is a seaport. |
| 225. sieve | A sieve will not hold water. |
| 226. Scandinavia | He looked as though he came from Scandinavia. |
| 227. slaughter | The cattle were taken to the slaughter house. |
| 228. stagnant | The water had become stagnant. |
| 229. scenery | The scenery was better than she had expected. |
| 230. sombrero | He wore the sombrero on the back of his head. |
| 231. smelting | One of the large industries is iron smelting. |
| 232. spindle | The spindle was held firmly between her fingers as she spun. |
| 233. sickle | He cut the grass with a sickle. |
| 234. terrace | The rice was grown on a terrace on the side of a mountain. |
| 235. stadium | The games were held in the stadium. |
| 236. sterile | He washed the wound until it was sterile. |
| 237. textile | He was an expert at the textile trade. |
| 238. sculpture | The building was decorated with sculpture. |
| 239. transplant | It is necessary to transplant rice. |
| 240. Socrates | Socrates was a great and famous Greek. |
| 241. transportation | Transportation was largely on horseback in those days. |
| 242. Sparta | Sparta was a famous Greek city. |
| 243. tillable | The soil was not tillable. |
| 244. stylus | They wrote with a stylus. |
| 245. thresher | The thresher separates the grain from the stalk and chaff. |

SPECIAL SPELLING TEST (*Continued*)

| *Word* | *Illustrative Sentence* |
|---|---|
| 246. Saxons | The Saxons were people who settled in England many centuries ago. |
| 247. warp | The board will not warp. |
| 248. tributary | The river had many tributaries. |
| 249. vitamin (e) | The vegetable contained an important vitamin. |
| 250. tulip | He picked a tulip and pinned it on his coat. |
| 251. scythe | The scythe cut the grain faster than a sickle. |
| 252. thatch | The house had a thick thatch on the roof. |
| 253. volcano | The volcano was not active. |
| 254. tunic | He wore a white tunic. |
| 255. stampede | She feared that the cattle would stampede. |
| 256. vineyard | They toiled long hours in the vineyard. |
| 257. sausage | He ate sausage nearly every day. |
| 258. silo | He filled the silo with food for the horses. |
| 259. wharves | The boat drew up along the wharves. |
| 260. tuberculin | Were the cows tuberculin tested? |

*Reliability of the Test.* Since the outcome of this experimental study is dependent upon the results obtained from the administration of the special spelling test, it is obviously necessary that the measuring instrument be reliable. The writer has attempted to show that the techniques used in the selection of the words were such as to make the test a comparable measure of the unusual words which the pupils might have acquired in the several experimental situations. The comparability of the lists has been supported by the ratings of frequency of occurrence given by Thorndike. The testing technique which was used was one which is commonly accepted. But what confidence can be placed in the results from the test? Are pupils' scores reliable evidence of their ability to spell the words in this sort of test situation or are the scores affected largely by chance?

In order to discover how consistent a measure the test afforded, the scores of a hundred children were selected at random. These scores were for the initial test at the beginning of the experiment and for the testing at the end of the first experimental period of five weeks. These two series of scores were correlated by the Pearson product-moment method. The obtained correlation, $r = .973 \pm .004$, is very high and permits entire confidence to be placed in the consistency of the measuring instrument. It should be noted that this high correlation was obtained after five weeks had elapsed during which the scores of the children were influenced by the experiment. The correlation which would have been

TABLE IX

*Reliability of Special Spelling Test Based on 100 Cases*

|  | Initial | After 5-Week Period |
|---|---|---|
| Mean .............. | 84.80 | 97.40 |
| S. D.$_M$ ............. | 2.49 | 2.74 |
| Number ........... | 100 | 100 |

$$r = .973 \pm .004$$

obtained had the test been repeated immediately after the first testing would have been at least as high and probably higher. The means and standard deviations of the series of scores upon which the correlation was based are shown in Table IX.

# IV

## Carrying Out the Study

AFTER the two counties in Maryland had been selected as the locale for the experimental study on the basis of their comparability of setting, there were three essential steps in carrying out the investigation. First, it was necessary to secure measurements of the sixth grade children of the factors which might conceivably be significant to the study as a basis for equating the several groups; second, the conditions of learning throughout the study had to be carefully formulated so that the groups would be in comparable learning situations except for the experimental factors being studied; and, third, it was necessary to have a measure of the children on the special spelling test at the beginning and end of the experimental period.

The experimental period covered the fifteen school weeks between March 2 and June 13 in 1931. The various measures needed for equating purposes were secured just previous to this period.

*Methods of Securing the Test Data.* Because of the relationship between reading and spelling it was believed necessary to have a reliable measure of reading ability. Since the experiment was concerned with the social studies field it was equally important to have an evaluation of achievement in this field. It is recognized that while reading comprehension is an ability which may be analyzed with reasonable exactness and measured with a fair degree of validity, measures in the social studies field, particularly at the time the study was undertaken, were not satisfactory. But a survey test limited to the measurement of the information possessed by the boys and girls in history and geography was available. Likewise it was possible to get a measure of spelling ability insofar as this is measured by a standardized test. And, of course, the intelligence scores of the children made on a standardized group intelligence test could be obtained with little difficulty. These various abilities were measured and the chronological ages of the children were recorded during February, 1931, such data as ages and mental ages being computed as of February 15th.

It is obvious, of course, that the four groups had to be equated also on the basis of the scores made on the first administration of the special spelling test, the construction of which has been described in the previous chapter. This test was given on the first two days of the experimental period, March 2 and 3.

The bases upon which the groups were equated, and the tests used in measuring these factors were as follows:

| | |
|---|---|
| Chronological age | Obtained from pupil's individual record card |
| Intelligence | Otis Self-Administering Test of Mental ability, Intermediate Examination, Form A |
| Reading achievement | New Stanford Achievement Battery, Advanced, Form V |
| History and civics | New Stanford Achievement Battery, Advanced, Form V |
| Geography | New Stanford Achievement Battery, Advanced, Form V |
| Spelling | New Stanford Achievement Battery, Advanced, Form V |
| Initial spelling score | Special Spelling Test |

*Scheduling the Units.* In order to distinguish the effects of the individual units, a schedule of the groups was worked out which rotated the order of the units in each of the three groups. This procedure also tends to counteract any constant influence which might be exerted if the units were studied always in the same order. In this schedule the spelling test was to be given during the first two days of the first five-week period; during the first two days of the second five-week period; and again at the close of the fifteen weeks of the experiment. Table X shows the arrangement as it was carried out.

The schools which were assigned to each of the three unit groups in County A had to be selected in such a manner as to make the groups as comparable as possible in such respects as relative pro-

TABLE X

*Schedule of Experimental Groups for Study of Effect of Social Studies Upon Children's Ability to Spell Unusual Words*

| Groups* | Initial Test | First Period | Second Testing | Second Period | Third Period | Final Testing |
|---|---|---|---|---|---|---|
| | March 2–3 | March 2 to April 3 | April 6–7 | April 6 to May 8 | May 11 to June 12 | June 15–16 |
| A-1 | | Cotton Unit | | Cereal Grain Unit | Domesticated Animals Unit | |
| A-2 | | Cereal Grain Unit | | Domesticated Animals Unit | Cotton Unit | |
| A-3 | | Domesticated Animals Unit | | Cotton Unit | Cereal Grain Unit | |
| B | | History and Geography | | History and Geography | History and Geography | |

* Groups A-1, A-2, and A-3 are three comparable groups in County A taking three social studies units in different order.

Group B is the comparable group in County B having history and geography as separate subjects.

portion of small-town and city schools; relative excellence of instruction; social and economic status of the school communities; and size of classes and other mechanical and administrative factors which conceivably might affect the results. In Chapter II there was described the comparability of County A and County B. In making up the groups within County A a similar type of equating was necessary. In selecting the schools for each group the judgment of the Assistant Superintendent of Schools was largely relied upon. This individual had had a long background of experience throughout the county and was thoroughly familiar not only with the schools but with the communities as well. The closeness with which test scores were approximated in the three groups, which will be shown later, is evidence of the reliability of the judgments.

After the selection of the groups early in February, teachers and principals were informed of the purpose of the investigation and the group to which they had been assigned by means of a letter which was sent out by the superintendent of schools. The letter (omitting the names of the schools) follows.

—————————, Maryland,
February 3, 1931.

My dear Principal:

You will be interested to know, I am sure, that a study is to be made of the effect upon pupils' spelling ability of certain of the social study units in the sixth grade. As a basis for improving the teaching of spelling it will be worthwhile to know just what effect, if any, teaching the social studies in the usual way with no special emphasis upon spelling has upon the ability to spell words which the pupils encounter in the units.

While more detailed instructions will be sent to you later, yet the schedule for the experiment can be given now. The Fruit Unit, a three weeks' unit for the sixth grade, will be taught in all schools for the three weeks ending February 27th.

The following units will be taught in the schools as indicated. It will be necessary to adhere strictly to the time schedule as shown for each school:

*Group 1.* (Names of 9 schools given.) Cotton Unit: March 2 to April 3; Cereal Grain Unit: April 6 to May 8; Domesticated Animals Unit: May 11 to June 12.

*Group 2.* (Names of 9 schools given.) Cereal Grain Unit: March 2 to April 3; Domesticated Animals Unit: April 6 to May 8; Cotton Unit: May 11 to June 12.

*Group 3.* (Names of 10 schools given.) Domesticated Animals Unit: March 2 to April 3; Cotton Unit: April 6 to May 8; Cereal Grain Unit: May 11 to June 12.

This study is being undertaken by Mr. I. Keith Tyler, of Teachers College, under the direction of Dr. H. B. Bruner. We ask the cooperation of every sixth grade teacher in order that this study may be carried out successfully. In order that the study may be as scientific as possible it will be necessary that any instructions that may be given be followed exactly.

Very sincerely yours,

—————————————

Superintendent

In County B the principals and teachers were informed by a similar letter which stated that a study was to be made of the effect upon pupils' spelling ability of the teaching of history and geography. It was indicated that the children would be tested three times but that otherwise regular work would proceed as usual. Cooperation was requested as in the letter above.

Following the sending of this letter the battery of tests was administered as indicated, followed, at the beginning of the experimental period, by the administration of the special spelling test. Accompanying this test was a sheet, which went to each teacher, in which were given the instructions to be followed during the study. The instructions were prepared so as to indicate the manner in which the teaching of spelling was to be conducted during the fifteen weeks in which the project was in operation.

*Spelling Instruction in the Two Counties.* The spelling text being used in both counties at this time was *Essentials of Spelling* by Pearson and Suzzallo.[1] Each county devoted a period not exceeding fifteen minutes daily to instruction in spelling. During the period of the investigation this spelling instruction was entirely restricted to the words actually given in the speller. It was assumed that this would prevent direct teaching of any of the words in the special spelling test since in the latter the commonest words were ruled out. A comparison of the lists reveals, however, that the word "minerals" which is in the special spelling test is also included in its singular form among the words for the second half of the sixth grade in the Pearson and Suzzallo speller. There are several reasons for believing that this repetition is inconsequential. In the first place, the list of words is long, 260 in all, and a single word is not a significant proportion. In the second place, the word, in its singular form, was taught in all the groups and tends to act as a constant rather than as a special factor in the experiment.

The procedure used during the regular spelling period in both counties was patterned after that which is advised by the authors of the speller in the "Directions for Teachers."[2] It was a drill procedure on both new and review words. The carry-over from the words taught in this manner to the new words on which no instruction was given was certainly not increased by any conscious activity on the part of the teachers. Nowhere in the "Directions for Teachers" do the authors suggest the use of rules or generalizations in teaching spelling; the book itself gives only four "spell-

[1] Henry Carr Pearson and Henry Suzzallo, *Essentials of Spelling, Middle Grades.* American Book Company, New York, 1921.
[2] *Ibid.*, pp. vii-xii.

ing rules" and these are presented on the last page in the book in the midst of such supplementary material as the hundred "spelling demons," the Ayres Scale, and the like.[3] Clearly, then, with the exception of the one word mentioned above the regular spelling instruction did not affect directly the ability of the pupils to spell the words in the special spelling test. What effect there was, if any, would be due to such generalization on the part of the pupils as might result from their experience with the words in the regular list. And as Carroll has pointed out, such generalization may be negative as well as positive.[4]

Many teachers attempt to deal with difficult words which children need to use in their written work by various devices in connection with the activity which is underway in the subject in which the need for the word arises. It would be expected that teachers in both counties would in a similar way be guiding the pupils in this experiment in learning to spell the very words upon which the study is based—the words peculiar to the subject matter of the units or subjects. In order to safeguard against just such efforts, so that the investigation might be limited purely to secondary learning, the sheet of instructions outlined the procedure to be used with regard to misspelled words, "drilling on words," and the like. The sheet which was sent out to all teachers engaged in the project was as follows:

### Instructions to Teachers Regarding Cooperation During the Experiment

During the period of this experiment teachers are asked to do no work with spelling except to have regular spelling lessons from *Essentials of Spelling* by Pearson and Suzzallo. No attempt is to be made to drill upon words that come up in the social studies units or in history and geography. Since the experiment is concerned with words which are not in the speller, the regular lessons are to be continued.

In pupils' compositions, board work, and other written work, where words are misspelled the pupil's attention is to be called to the *correct spelling* of the word, but he should not be drilled on this. We are trying to find out if pupils *will* learn to spell words incidentally.

The tests are not to be discussed with the pupils after they have been

[3] *Ibid.*, p. 84.
[4] Herbert Allen Carroll, *Generalization of Bright and Dull Children; A Comparative Study with Special Reference to Spelling.* Bureau of Publications, Teachers College, Columbia University, New York, 1930.

given except to point out that most of the words are quite difficult and thus to encourage pupils who may have felt that they have done badly. The words that are tested upon should not be recalled.

Teachers are to teach the units, the geography, and history, as they always teach except for the omission of spelling work as above. Teachers need not worry or concern themselves with the results of the tests so far as the pupils are concerned since the investigation is undertaken only to find out whether or not pupils do learn some words incidentally in connection with the social studies work.

*Social Studies Instruction in the Two Counties.* It has been shown that the direct teaching of spelling was definitely limited and that the spelling textbook and the methods of teaching the subject in the two counties were the same. Likewise, the time devoted to social studies in County A was equal to that in County B which was devoted to history and geography. In the first county a single period of one and one-half hours was set aside for the learning activities in connection with the units; in the second county forty-five minutes was scheduled for geography and a similar time allotment made for history. In both situations this time was usually taken during the morning session though individual teachers sometimes varied this arrangement. In a like manner some of the teachers devoted somewhat more or somewhat less than the scheduled time to the instruction in both counties. In general, however, the time devoted to teaching the social studies in County A and County B was equal.

The principal difference between the situations in the two places was in relation to the way in which learning was organized. Roughly, the comparison is between teaching logically organized subjects and teaching with the unit organization in a broad field. What this means in terms of emphasis, subject matter, activities, and intended outcomes will be described in detail.

*Subjects vs. Units.* This is not the place for an extended treatment of all the varying concepts of a "unit" or a "unit of work." An excellent description of the various types of units found in American schools is given in a pamphlet by Bruner.[5] Nor is it the

[5] Herbert B. Bruner, *The Place of Units in Course of Study Construction.* South Dakota Curriculum Revision Program, Bulletin No. 2. State Department of Education, Pierre, South Dakota, 1930.

place for a lengthy exposition of the various points of view regarding the place of school subjects in the curriculum. It is necesary, rather, that the terms here used be defined in relation to the major problem of the contrast between subject organization and unit organization in the two situations with which this study is concerned.

A "subject," then, as it is used here may be defined as a generally accepted, formalized subdivision of study. Thus arithmetic, spelling, history, or algebra would be a subject as here considered. It is clear that history and geography are both subjects because they are generally accepted as such; each has a formalized organization, and each is a rather clearly defined subdivision of study. It is quite true that the boundaries of even the most traditional subjects become difficult to fix as one delves into the areas which border upon other subjects. At what point, for example, does arithmetic merge into geometry? Or physics into chemistry? But within the somewhat uncertain boundaries there is a great deal of material which is clearly recognized as belonging to a particular subject.

A "broad field" may be defined as consisting of an area of study which embraces several related subjects. The field of science, for example, includes botany, astronomy, physics, chemistry and a host of other subjects in the natural and physical field. Again, social studies, as it is thought of in County A, covers such subjects as history, geography, civics, and others of a similar nature. Compton, in writing of social studies as an elementary school subject, says that it includes history, geography, civics, and economics,

. . . . and deals with the problems confronting people who live in social groups and interprets the relation existing between the physical world and the various modes of living. It is concerned with those phases of life activities and interests which relate directly to the organization and development of the social order and to man as a member of social groups. Social studies embodies those experiences which help us understand what human beings are doing, what they have done in the past, and, perhaps, what they will do in the future. These experiences are designed to promote understanding of living conditions, appreciations of their possibilities, and knowledge adequate to make worthy living possible.[6]

[6] Lillian Compton. "The Social Studies in the Elementary School," p. 14. *Curriculum Revision Program, Allegany County, Maryland.* Allegany County Public Schools, Cumberland, Maryland, 1930. (*mimeographed.*)

In summarizing, the purpose of the social studies is the cultivation of right civic ideals and attitudes, the development of right civic habits and skills, the establishment of a usable fund of knowledge and the understanding of some elementary principles underlying modern civilization.[7]

It should be noted in these two statements that the area included within Compton's concept of social studies is the broad field of human relations, past and present. The purpose of teaching social studies as she conceives it is to develop certain desirable habits, attitudes, and understandings, but it is apparent that these are presumed to come from the study of the social studies field.

Since unit organization is being contrasted with subject organization it is well, too, to have a clear conception of a "unit" as it is used in this study. A unit is a block of experience organized with relation to some unifying element—a generalization, a problem, an aesthetic appreciation, a skill to be acquired. It is not a logically organized block of subject matter. It becomes a unit only when the learners are having experiences in relation to the unifying element, and these experiences are organized not in relation to the inherent logic of the subject matter but, ideally, at least, according to the psychology of the learning process itself. It is unified because the learners are having a series of experiences which are related by the "large understanding" they are presumed to be developing, the problem they are presumed to be solving, the aesthetic appreciation they are presumed to be coming to feel, or the skill they are presumed to be acquiring.

A unit may be within a subject, within a field, or as broad as life itself. The units with which this investigation deals are "generalization units" within the broad field of social studies. This term implies that a generalization or understanding was the unifying element of each unit and that the experiences which were related were all within the area of study that is included in the field of social studies. This type of unit, also called a "unit of understanding," is described by Bruner as follows:

. . . By unit of understanding is meant a unit so organized that everything that is included in the way of content, the organization itself, and the method of presenting it to the class is for the purpose of

[7] *Ibid.*, p. 15.

making it possible for the child to grasp the big understanding or theme that is back of it. It therefore includes not only the facts, incidents, informations, vicarious and personal experiences and the emotional interpretations that the course of study writer selects but also the theme itself as the most important factor in the unit. In such a unit the facts and informations selected as assimilative material are secondary in importance to the understanding of the theme. They are chosen because they have particular value in revealing to the pupils the truth of the generalization that holds central place in the mind of the teacher. The theme becomes the organizing factor determining the exclusion of some material and inclusion of other although this often seems to violate the principle of logical and traditional unity previously used.[8]

In the subject type of organization the subject matter and the learning activities in which the children participate are generally limited by the boundaries of the traditional concepts of the field with which the subject is concerned. In a strict subject type of organization, for example, children studying arithmetic might learn about the keeping of a family budget and have considerable practice in the computations and simple book-keeping which this involves. To extend this, however, into the interrelationships of family budgets and standards of living, and thence to delve into the causes of poverty and unemployment as they are related to low standards of living, would clearly be going beyond the subject.

With the unit organization within a broad field the subject matter and activities are limited principally by their relevancy to the unifying factor and the area of the broad field. A generalization unit aimed to develop the understanding that "people move from place to place in search of higher standards of living" might be developed around the general theme of the Westward Movement in this country. Its subject matter would be broader than history and would include material from geography and civics as well, and involve activities associated with such subjects as spelling, handwriting, drama, oral and written composition, and art.

It should be made clear that this study was not contrasting a completely traditional organization of instruction with a wholly progressive child-centered one. Rather do we have on the one hand logical subject organization which has been modified by attempts to meet child interest, and on the other a type of organiza-

[8] Bruner, *op. cit.*, p. 10.

tion which has sacrificed strict subject organization in order to develop certain primary objectives, in this case large concepts. In the latter situation the material is organized in units which are more nearly psychological than logical in their arrangement, but which fall short of being really progressive in their emphasis on the past, in their observance of the limits of the broad field, and in their preoccupation with "described" rather than "first-hand" experience. It would be well to examine, then, the contrasts between the two in terms of the courses of study, the subject matter, and the activities of the pupils.

*The Courses of Study.* The courses of study which presumably were used by the teachers as a guide to teaching were very different in the two situations. In County B the courses of study in history and geography were chiefly characterized by their brevity while the course of study in County A for this period consisted of three voluminous units.

"Our Old-World Heritage" is the title of the mimeographed course of study in history. During the experiment the work covered included a study of the Greeks and the Romans and their contributions to our civilization. No objectives are stated nor are the learning activities suggested, the course being called a "General Topical Outline" and consisting of a succession of topics each followed by a series of references to the principal textbooks. A sample from the outline under the main heading of "II. What we owe to the Greeks and Romans," is given in order to reveal the type of guidance which was afforded the teacher in handling the subject matter.

C. How Greece came to her Golden Age and spread her ideas through the world.
    1. The Athenians made their city the strongest power in Greece.
        *a.* The rebuilding of Athens—The Acropolis, the Parthenon.
        *b.* Athens at its height—"The Age of Pericles."
            1) Sculptors and architects—Phidias.
            2) Wise men and great leaders—Pericles and Aristides.

Paginated references:
Bourne and Benton, *Introductory American History*, pp. 24-30.
Burnham, *Our Beginnings in Europe and America*, pp. 65-67.
Gordy, *American Beginnings in Europe*, pp. 28-35.

Hall, *Men of Old Greece*, pp. 171-217.
Hall, *Our Ancestors in Europe*, pp. 59-61.
Woodburn and Moran, *Introduction to American History*, pp. 44-49.

2. Some great men of Athens added their names to the glowing glory of Greece.
   *a.* A great teacher—Socrates and his school.
   *b.* Great writers and public speakers—Herodotus and Demosthenes.
   *c.* Greek plays and Greek singers—the theatre of Dionysius.

Paginated references:
Atkinson, *An Introduction to American History*, pp. 49-51.
Bourne and Benton, *Introductory American History*, p. 33.
Burnham, *Our Beginnings in Europe and America*, pp. 67-72.
Gordy, *American Beginnings in Europe*, pp. 35-37, 43-46.
Hall, *Men of Old Greece*, pp. 221-263.
Hall, *Our Ancestors in Europe*, pp. 21, 39, 48.
Woodburn and Moran, *Introduction to American History*, pp. 30-43.

3. A youthful king of Macedon turns the world into a Greek empire.
   *a.* Jealousy between Sparta and Athens.
   *b.* Philip of Macedon, master of all Greece.
   *c.* Alexander's conquest in the East.
   *d.* Greek ideas extended into the Persian world by Alexander, the Great.
   *e.* The world becomes Greek.

Paginated references:
Bourne and Benton, *Introductory American History*, pp. 42-44.
Burnham, *Our Beginnings in Europe and America*, pp. 72-73.
Gordy, *American Beginnings in Europe*, pp. 47-54.
Hall, *Our Ancestors in Europe*, pp. 61-70.
Woodburn and Moran, *Introduction to American History*, pp. 58-66.[9]

In order to indicate the approximate subject matter which was covered in the course of study for the period during which the experimental project was under way, the chief headings of the logically outlined material on the Greeks and Romans are given. The amount of detail which was given under each of these headings may be noted from the fact that the section quoted in complete form was the material which was included under a single heading. The principal headings:

II. What we owe to the Greeks and Romans.
   A. How the Greeks became the first civilized nation in Europe.
   B. How the Greeks saved freedom for the world.

[9] *Our Old-World Heritage,* a mimeographed course of study used in County B. No author or publisher given. No date. pp. 2-3.

C. How Greece came to her Golden Age and spread her ideas
through the world.
D. What the Greeks gave to us.
E. How Rome became the conqueror of Greece and how Greek
learning conquered Rome.
F. How Rome grew into an empire and ruled a Roman world.
G. What the Romans gave to the world.[10]

For guidance in teaching the geography the teachers in County
B used an outline prepared in one of the state normal schools. In
this material the subject matter is laid out in lessons with a single
statement which is referred to as a "problem" and "lesson objective" for each lesson. No references are given and the subject
matter outline becomes a series of these single-sentence objectives.
As an example of what such a course gives, the problem-objectives
under the heading "France" are given in complete form:

### France

1. To understand the location of France at the "crossroads of Europe." (Map Study).
2. To understand the location of Paris as the heart of France.
3. To appreciate the artistic leadership of Paris.
4. To understand the balance of agriculture and manufacturing in
France.
5. To understand the diversity of agriculture in France.
6. To understand the character of manufacturing and the location
of the manufacturing districts.
7. To understand the location of the iron industry and its relation to Germany.
8. To understand the fishing industry of St. Malo.
9. To understand the location of the port of Marseilles.
10. To understand the relation of France to her African colonies.
11. To understand the character of the trade of France.

In a similar fashion fifteen of these statements of objectives are
given for the study of Germany and twenty-two for the study of
Russia and Siberia. In addition seven "special problems" are given
in outline for Russia and Siberia. These problems are topic statements. Two examples are: "The Natural and Cultural Unit of
Russia" and "The Political Experiment of New Russia."

From the above description and examples of the courses of
study used in County B there should be sufficient evidence to support the following conclusions regarding them:

[10] *Op. cit.*

1. These courses give little or no aid to the teacher in formulating the general goals of her teaching.

2. These courses give no help in the selection of learning activities except insofar as the references given in history suggest reading on the part of the pupils.

3. The courses place chief emphasis on subject matter, selected chiefly from the point of view of its value to adults.

4. A logical order of learning is presumed to be followed by the pupils.

5. Subject matter and activities are confined almost entirely to the conventional limits of the subject.

The three units which constitute the course of study for the fifteen weeks in County A were much more extensive in character. They, too, are mimeographed, but contain a much greater variety of materials. It has already been indicated that these units are "generalization" or "theme" units; that is, that each is organized around a central theme or broad understanding which is the unifying element. Presumably the subject matter and learning activities are chosen because of the promise which they give of revealing to pupils the central theme. Or, to put it another way, those content materials and pupil activities are suggested which give opportunity for the pupil to develop the "key understanding" for which the unit is to be taught.

It would be well, therefore, to present in broad outline the manner in which the social studies program in this country is organized so that the reader may grasp the connection of the unit themes with the larger understandings which underlie the entire elementary school social studies. Chart I gives the scheme for the sixth grade, showing the controlling themes or "large understandings," the particular aspects of these themes which are developed, and the specific units which develop the particular aspects. The five themes of Interdependence, Control, Adaptation, Migration and Democracy, around which these units are organized, are those which are used for the entire elementary social studies program. The assumption is made that these are the basic "key understandings" which enable an individual to interpret past and present experience in an intelligible fashion. The place of the three units with

CHART I. AN OUTLINE OF THE SOCIAL STUDIES PROGRAM IN
THE SIXTH GRADE OF COUNTY A

| Controlling Theme* | Aspect of Theme Which Is Developed in Unit | Unit Title |
| --- | --- | --- |
| Interdependence | Interdependence Has Been Made Possible Through Development of Communication | Binding the Nations Together Through the Development of Means of Communication |
| Control | Man's Increasing Control Over Distance | The Swift Development of Transportation in Recent Years |
| | Man's Increasing Control Over the Water Supply | Opening New Agricultural Areas Through the Development of Irrigation |
| Adaptation | The Tendency of the Physical Environment to Determine the Industries of the People | The Fruit Industry—A Factor in the Standard of Living |
| | The Tendency of the Physical Environment to Determine Modes and Standards of Living | The Cereal Grains—An Important Factor in Determining Types of Civilization |
| | The Tendency of the Physical Environment to Determine Industry | Domesticated Animals — A Factor in the Standard of Living |
| Migration | The Tendency of People to Seek New Lands for a Higher Standard of Living | Early American Life—An Adventure in the Conquest of Free Land |
| Democracy | The Tendency of People to Demand Economic Democracy | The Influence of Cotton Upon the Development of Our Country |

* Complete statements of themes are:
   Interdependence: Groups are becoming increasingly interdependent upon one another.
   Control: Man is gaining an increasing control over nature.
   Adaptation: It is necessary for man to adapt himself to meet the requirements of nature.
   Migration: Man has a tendency to move from place to place in search of better conditions of living.
   Democracy: Man inevitably struggles toward democracy.

which this study is concerned—the Cotton Unit, the Domesticated Animals Unit, and the Cereal Grains Unit—may be seen from this chart.[11]

An examination of the course of study units themselves reveals that they are organized according to a common pattern. The three elements which are usually considered necessary in a good course of study are included; namely, objectives, content or subject matter, and learning activities. In addition there are many other features which are added on the assumption that they give additional help and guidance to the teacher. These may be classified under seven headings:

1. *Objectives.* At the beginning of each of the units there is presented a statement of the goals which the teacher should have in mind as the desirable outcomes from the study of the unit. These objectives include the statement of the general theme or understanding which is to be developed; subordinate generalizations which are likely to grow out of the work of the unit; and a series of detailed statements of skills, facts, and information, and attitudes and appreciations which are presumed to be acquired.

2. *Suggested approaches.* In this section there are listed a number of activities which the teacher may use in getting the unit started. They are ways of stimulating an interest on the part of the pupils in the unit, of raising questions and problems which the children will be likely to want to solve, and of giving a hasty preview of the unit.

3. *Suggested activities.* A large group of learning activities and pupil experiences are suggested from which the teacher may choose those which seem most appropriate to the interests and abilities of her group. These involve "intellectual" activities of various sorts and "expressive" or "creative" activities which afford children an opportunity for using abilities of various other sorts. They include a group called "culminating activities," from which the teacher may develop a comprehensive activity as the final and culminating part of the work of the unit.

4. *The overview.* Each unit contains an "overview" which ap-

[11] In setting up this scheme, the themes were looked upon as major emphases, but the interrelationship of all the themes was recognized with regard to any of the units.

pears to be a general summary of the point of view of the unit showing the contribution which it makes to the development of the theme. It is intended for the use of the teacher in seeing the relation of the unit to the entire social studies program.

5. *Content materials.* A logical arrangement of the subject matter covered in the unit is given in this section. It is arranged in outline form and each principal section includes a series of pupil references. The teacher is cautioned that this logical sequence is not to be thought of as the order in which the material is to be learned; rather it is said to be a sort of check list for determining worthwhile subject matter and a means of finding references when pupils are engaged in activity involving a particular section of the subject matter.

6. *Suggested means for evaluating.* This section is included in two of the three units. It is a summarizing check list of the kinds of "growth" which the children should have made as a result of the activity of the unit.

7. *Bibliography.* In addition to the references which are given throughout the outline of the content of each unit, there is an extensive general bibliography for the use of the teacher and as a source of possible material for pupils.

With this general form of the units in mind, it is well next to examine a sampling of the material included under each of the headings. Obviously the units are too extensive to give in detail; enough will be presented to permit the drawing of general conclusions only.

The controlling themes of each of the units were as follows:

Cereal Grains Unit—Standards of living and type of civilization are determined largely by physical environment.
Cotton Unit—Democracy progresses inevitably with the tendency of people to demand economic democracy.
Domesticated Animals Unit—The physical environment tends to determine the major industry of a region.[12]

Obviously these objectives are expressed in adult terms. What is expected, apparently, is that the pupils shall develop a comparable

[12] These and the other excerpts from the units are taken from the course of study units used in County A. Their source may be obtained from the author on request.

*understanding,* though the words in which such a generalization on their part might be expressed would undoubtedly be vastly different from these which are set forth in the units.

Various subordinate generalizations which are given as objectives in the units include:

Cereal Grains Unit—
  1. Climate is an important determiner of the plant and animal life of any given region.
  2. Regions that supply men's needs with minimum expenditure of energy fail to develop characteristics and habits conducive to progress.
  3. Agriculture is the basis of permanent prosperity.

Cotton Unit—
  1. Cotton manufacturing may be carried on near or at long distances from where cotton is grown.
  2. Cotton has been a great economic factor in the development of our country.
  3. Cotton is more widely used for the making of cloth than any other material.

Domesticated Animals Unit—
  1. The farm animals supply civilization with three great needs: food, clothing, and power.
  2. The occupations of people are the most powerful factors in determining their modes of living.
  3. Materials of the meat packing industry formerly considered waste are now, through the work of modern science, being used to serve some need.

Several of the specific objectives which are stated in terms of information and attitudes are presented. These are stated in the usual infinitive form as "to learn," "to appreciate," etc. The Domesticated Animals Unit gives eight of these; the Cereal Grains Unit, twelve; and the Cotton Unit, twenty-two. The majority of these are factual, though some imply a more generalized type of understanding:

To gain some appreciation of the relation of the cotton industry to events leading to the Civil War.
To know the various uses of cotton.
To gain a conception of the speed with which cloth is manufactured.
To learn the chief areas of consumption of the wheat crop and the reasons.
To learn why the people of wheat producing and consuming regions have a dominant influence in civilization.

To learn the methods used in rice and wheat cultivation and the differences between the two.

To become familiar with the chief steps in the process of marketing
the animals, slaughtering the animals, and making the different
by-products.

To learn about the life of the cowboys and sheep herders.

Approaches, as given in the units, are ways that the teacher may
use to introduce the unit to a class. In each case five approaches
are suggested from which the teacher may choose the one most
appropriate to the group, or she may develop one of her own.
Sample approaches:

A visit to a dairy farm near your school gives opportunities to observe the breeds of cows, the plan of the barn, the food for the cows,
cleanliness with which milking is done, and the labor required. Such an
excursion will cause questions to be asked that will open up the unit.

A story given by a member of the class on some phase of animal life
during story telling period may tend to stimulate interest in further
study of animal life.

Reading to the class a description of a typical meal in a United
States home and one in China or Java, discussing the differences in
food, in service, etc.

Each child listing his menu for the preceding day (three meals)
turning these lists over to a committee whose duty it is to find the
food most commonly mentioned in these ninety to one hundred meals.
Wheat bread will probably be the food. From this might come a discussion of the necessity of wheat to us here in America and the vast
number of people who do not use wheat.

Reading together a story or book that will supply a common background of information and that will open up possibilities of planning
the work to be done in connection with the unit.

Studying interesting pictures of plantation life; cotton growing,
manufacturing, etc.

The activities suggested in the three units are organized differ-
ently in each unit. In the Domesticated Animals Unit they are
classified into four types with from six to twenty-five activities
given under each type. The four classifications together with
sample activities under each are:

1. Activities that help the children get skills, informations, appreciations and understandings.
   a. A class may be able to make an excellent collection of by-products
      derived from each of the animals.
   b. Showing how science has made it possible for all the animals to
      be utilized, a chart may be made listing each part of the animal

and showing what products are produced from these different parts of the carcass.

  c. Drawing a map showing the settler's grazing area during and after the "Westward Movement," and grazing areas of today.
  d. Visiting a museum to observe the evolution of the horse.
2. Activities that give pupils practice in using ideas, habits and information previously acquired.
  a. Having a class discussion on the topic: If all industries employed the vast number of persons the beef and cattle industry does, there would be no unemployment problem.
  b. Making a booklet of story or poem collections about the animal you are most interested in. Reading them to the class that their worth may be evaluated. Note if they are picturesque, contain good choice of words, easily read and understood.
  c. Making a series of pictures contrasting dairying in America by the colonists and dairying today.
  d. Making a piece of wool into a piece of yarn by washing, rinsing, drying, carding, combing and twisting.
3. Activities that encourage pupils to express their ideas and feelings.
  a. Writing a poem or song of the isolated, lonely life of a rancher on the vast plain.
  b. Making pictures that will express the child's idea of a grazing area, of a cattle ranch or a sheep ranch, depicting its vastness and openness.
  c. Composing a conversation between:
      Cowboys around the campfire.
      Cowboys during the round-up.
      The seller and buyer at the stockyard.
  d. Using clay to model a modern train used in transporting animals to show that they are humanely cared for.
4. Possible culminating activities.
  a. The class might prepare an assembly program using materials they have found that would be interesting—reading literature, original stories, original poems, dramatic conversations, tableaux and songs that can be used for a mixed program.
  b. If an exhibit has been collected, a talk to explain it to another group would be interesting.
  c. A book or booklets might be compiled from reports, collections, and drawings made. It could be left in the school or general library.

In the Cereal Grains Unit the activities are grouped with the corresponding subject matter in three large divisions. They are not classified according to type. The three divisions of content are: (1) the distribution of people upon the earth, (2) monsoon countries and rice cultivation, and (3) the area of cyclonic storms and wheat productions. In a sense each of these divisions is treated as a sub-unit. The activities given in connection with each sub-unit are unorganized, are many in number (in the first there are about 30 given; in the second, 120; and in the third, 180), and differ greatly in quality. Inspection reveals many of them to be similar to the "exercises" in textbooks; others are of the activity-school type. Twenty taken at random from the three lists are given here:

Read to find out how many people inhabit the earth.

Read to find the characteristics of monsoon climates.

Make a list of all the countries that are similar with respect to the items of temperature; of rainfall; of winds.

Find pictures that will show the differences in climate in the monsoon regions and the regions of cyclonic storms.

Read to find out under what climatic and surface conditions rice may best be cultivated.

List the countries suitable for rice culture.

Get pictures of rice plants in various stages of growth.

Write a description of a rice farm.

Make a floor piece showing the paddy fields ready for water showing various kinds of work going on; dress dolls to represent native costumes.

Discuss the kinds of traits one must have to be a successful rice farmer, and why.

Make a cartoon showing an American attempting to use modern machinery on a Chinese rice farm.

Read and discuss how mountains help in rice farming; how rivers help.

Find pictures giving illustrations of modes of living or of living conditions.

Discuss the size of the wheat farms of the United States and the size of rice farms in the Orient.

Read to find interesting incidents of what science has found out about wheat raising.

Collect newspaper clippings and magazine articles about Argentina.

Describe a modern flour mill that you have visited.

Make a relief map showing the surface features of Russia. Study the rainfall and climate problems from this map.

Read to find out what one needs in a diet to make him well and energetic.

Make an exhibit that will show the relative variety of foods in each of the three climates studied: the monsoon climate, the subtropical climate, and the cyclonic storm climates.

In the Cotton Unit a major activity, holding a cotton exposition, is suggested. The minor activities are divided according to subject matter in a similar fashion to the arrangement in the unit just discussed. The number of these activities is much less, however. There are five divisions of the content of the unit. The five, together with the number of activities suggested for each are: (1) Important Cotton Areas—12; (2) Interesting History of the Cotton Area—34; (3) The Production and Marketing of Cotton—13; (4) Methods and Extent of Cotton Manufacture—10; and (5) Importance and Scope of the Cotton Industry—10. These activities are very similar to those given in the Cereal Grains Unit. A sample of ten are given below to show their similarity, though dealing with different subject matter:

> Read materials giving information as to where cotton is produced in our country and in other countries.
> List the conditions necessary for the production of cotton.
> Illustrate by drawings, paintings, and booklets the life on a Southern plantation.
> Dramatize scenes as found on a plantation.
> List uses made of cotton during the World War.
> Paint an historical frieze showing the outstanding events in the history of cotton.
> Dramatize a scene at the Cotton Exchange.
> Make a chart showing the various uses of cotton (a) in the home (b) in industry.
> Make a collection of the by-products of cotton.
> On an outline map of Great Britain, indicate cities that are important for cotton manufacturing.

The overviews in the three units are one-page summaries of the point of view which dominates the unit. The relation of the theme, content, and activities is indicated. It is intended for the teacher in orienting her to the unit.

The subject matter of all three units is presented in the form of running outlines. Because the units were new to the teachers, it was felt necessary to give this content in considerable detail. From a half to two-thirds of each unit is given over to this factual material. It should be recognized that the material covered by each unit is not to be found similarly organized in any one textbook. Just because the content is gathered from so many sources, it became imperative that the teacher be able to see it as a whole; so that she might be able to sense the relationship among the various blocks of subject matter which go to make up the unit. This purpose the outline of content serves. It also provides a convenient way for the teacher to discover when the children are going too far afield. While no one teacher may cover all the subject matter, nor is she expected to, each teacher feels the need for some guide through the complexity of the mass of content.

A section of the running outline from each unit will reveal the nature of the content as it was presented to the teacher.

*Domesticated Animals Unit*—A paragraph from "Grazing in South America" which in turn is a subdivision of "Stock Raising for our Meat Supply."

2. Life on a ranch of a Pampas: Ranches called estancia; usually in shape of square; sometimes covers 10 degrees of square miles of land; capable of grazing 150,000 cattle, 100,000 sheep; requires labor of 500 men; owners often build Spanish-type homes around court or patio; used as flower garden; owner of ranch seldom lives on ranch; lives in large city or foreign country; wishes to be near school or church or stores or in social group; farmer rents estate; pays with part of crops; behind owner's house, rude huts of gauchos, Spanish-Indian bred cowboys; at age of four cowboy learns to ride; uses lasso or balo as plaything; catches birds, dogs; as he grows older he chases animals on horseback; becomes reckless rider; lives out-of-doors in sun, wind, rain; meat cooked in skin; tea main drink of cowboy; carries sheet knife; used in cutting meat when far from ranch house; costume striking; broad brim Spanish sombrero; bloomer like trousers tucked into boots; carries blanket or poncho round waist; used when necessary to sleep out-of-doors; plains dotted with little homes of workmen; usually occupied by Italians; 2,000,000 Italians came to Argentina to make fortune; homes rude mud huts; ranch overseen by agent; requires 2 or 3 days to visit all workmen's camps; many use airplanes; estancia sold by square hogne (6,000 acres) fenced into small pastures.

*Cereal Grains Unit*—A paragraph from "Rice Culture Methods" which in turn is a subdivision of the section on "Rice."

Methods of lowland rice culture: In densely populated regions where land is scarce, more careful methods used; fields used for centuries; wet variety of rice grown because of its greater and more certain yield; small fields of Orient preclude use of machinery and plentiful supply of cheap labor reduces necessity for it; some assistance from cattle and water buffalo; in United States, fields of 20 to 100 acres planted and harvested by machinery; rice demands many hands and continuous work; preparation of field requires minute care; field divided into series of flat basins which must receive water and retain it for eight to ten days; each basin shut in by embankments which must be kept in repair; ground in each basin plowed and harrowed; rice sowed; fields then covered with water for twenty or thirty days, being renewed at intervals so that it does not become stagnant and foul; when rice has sprung up, it is transplanted; this is very hard and unhealthful work; when transplanted into basins it is watered at intervals; these need careful supervision; when ripe, field must be drained before harvest begins; rice is cut with a sickle; husking is also done by hand and is slow work; grain put on bamboo frames to dry; threshed by drawing rice grass through a slit in a board thus pulling the grains from the heads and allowing them to fall into a receptacle; grain at this stage called a "paddy" as it has close fitting husk such as the oat has; kernel keeps much better unhusked so that husking is done at time of use; husking the paddy is daily task of oriental people; common sound throughout the Orient is the pounding of a heavy pestle in a vessel full of paddy thus removing the husks.

*Cotton Unit*—A section titled "Early Methods of Manufacturing" from the subject matter on "Methods and Extent of Cotton Manufacture."

Carding: First process is "carding"; this done with two brushes with wooden backs and wire teeth; a piece of raw cotton placed on one; with both brushes, cotton is mixed back and forth, straightened, disentangled, and finally shaped into soft, round roll.

Spinning: Spinning wheel—a spindle turned by a wheel; wheel turned so as to make spindle revolve rapidly; spinner holds one end of loose roll of "carded" cotton in hand, fastens other end to spindle; as spindle revolves, roll is drawn out and twisted into thread; process repeated until thread is firm and strong.

Weaving: Thread woven into cloth on loom made of four upright pieces of timber; two back posts connected by a piece called "yard beam"; "warp" or lengthwise threads wound around the "yard beam"; two front posts connected by piece of timber called "cloth beam"; around this, cloth is wound as it is woven. (Good descriptions of hand looms with clear illustrations found in Bonser and Mossman, *Industrial Arts for Elementary Grades,* pp. 145 and 181 and in Turpin, *Cotton,* p. 49.)

The Cereal Grains Unit and the Domesticated Animals Unit each contain a section with the heading "Suggestions for Evaluating the Teaching of This Unit." In a page or two there are presented pertinent questions by which the teacher may gauge the growth of the class in the objectives of the unit. A random selection of material from each of the units follows:

From the *Cereal Grain Unit:*

A. Have the pupils by their interests and activities manifested some growth in an attitude of tolerance toward—

1. The agricultural class of people?
3. The yellow race and the civilizations they have developed?
Have they gained some appreciation of—
    1. The stimulation of progress in the temperate cyclonic regions?
    5. The effect of rice cultivation on the character of the people engaged in it?
    9. The fact that rice production is the only means of supporting a dense agricultural population.
B. Have your pupils an understanding of such things as—
    2. The effect of climate on diet?
    8. The methods used in the cultivation of rice and of wheat and how they differ?
    9. The requirements of a good diet?
C. Do your pupils know—
    4. The methods of preparing rice and wheat for consumption?
    9. The fundamental differences in the diet of different climatic regions?
    11. The chief avenues and methods of transportation of cereals?
D. Have the following terms taken on definite meanings?
    Cereals, monsoons, . . . civilization, . . . standard of living, . . . rural population, urban population, . . . industrial regions, . . . cheap labor, . . . labor saving machinery, . . . erosion, exhausted land, . . . intensive farming, . . . prevailing winds, . . . transportation facilities, . . . malnutrition, . . . rotation of crops.
E. Have your pupils grown in such habits and skills as—
    1. Reading to acquire definite information?
    3. Making a talk before the class on some topic prepared individually or by a group?
    8. Interpreting maps, charts, tables, graphs, etc.?
    11. Working cooperatively in a group?
    15. Taking intelligent part in class discussion?
    19. Formulating and carrying out their own plan of study?
    21. Explaining and interpreting constructed and illustrative material?

From the *Domesticated Animals Unit:*

A. Have your pupils by their interests and activities manifested some growth in an attitude of appreciation and tolerance toward—
    1. The effort of science, invention and man's intelligence to develop better animal breeds, increase the size of the herd, increase the meatpacking industry, skin, butter, cheese, and wool production to supply the increasing population?
    3. The hardships and habits of living of the ranchmen and sheep herders?

B. The Unit gives opportunities for further development of many concepts. Have such terms as the following taken on definite meaning?

Ranches or estancia or stations, markets and marketing, meat packing, by-products, preservation of food, surplus produce, consumption, arable land, related industries, breeds, mountain pasture and plain pasture?

C. Have your pupils grown in such habits and skills as—
  1. Reading to acquire definite informations?
  3. Making a talk before the class on some topic prepared individually or by a group?
  4. Making charts, graphs, and pictographs to express information?
  6. Collecting, classifying and evaluating materials?
  11. Reading good stories for information?

D. Do your pupils know—
  1. Location of the great animal producing regions?
  3. Names and locations of a few important meat-packing, wool manufacturing, and leather manufacturing centers, and harbors used for importation and exportation of the articles?
  6. The characteristics of each of the animal producing regions?
  7. The outstanding features in the lives of shepherds and cowboys?

Each of the three units contains an extensive bibliography. In the Cereal Grains Unit and the Domesticated Animals Unit the references are for both the teacher and the pupils, while in the Cotton Unit there are separate lists of references; one for pupils and one for the teacher. In all three units the lists of readings are extensive. There are over eighty separate books listed in the Domesticated Animals Unit; seventy are listed in the Cereal Grains Unit; and the Cotton Unit gives thirty-six listings for the pupils and twelve additional listings for the teacher. These references in the three units refer to history textbooks, to geographies, to readers, to encyclopedias, to works of children's fiction, to informational types of books for children, to United States Government bulletins, and to various other types of materials which contain the necessary facts and background of the unit and which may be obtained for the pupils. Here, again, is an outstanding contrast with the situation in the county in which history and geography were being taught as separate subjects. In County B there were textbooks in each subject and little additional material was referred to in the course of study; in County A there were no textbooks and a great variety of references were given, each classroom and school being provided with a variety of books instead of a set or two of textbooks.

As with the courses of study in history and geography it is possible from this inspection of the units in social studies to draw certain conclusions:

1. The units set forth the general goal of each unit in terms of a major generalization and suggest other goals for the teacher in terms of other types of learning outcomes.

2. The units are generous in their suggestion of learning activities in which children may engage in order to achieve the objectives. But these activities tended to be concerned with described rather than first-hand experience and are highly verbalistic in character.

3. The units place a great deal of emphasis upon subject matter but subordinate it to the achievement of the "large understanding." Subject matter is looked upon as the means rather than as the end. The content appears to have been suggested largely from the point of view of its value for adults rather than for children, just as in the case of the history and geography, but the teacher is given greater freedom to choose from the subject matter suggested that which will appeal most to the needs and interests of her pupils.

4. No particular order of activities is presumed to be followed in the units. The only order suggested is in terms of the major activities; that is, an approach activity, a series of general activities, and a culminating or summary activity. Otherwise a teacher can arrange the activities in terms of the individual peculiarities of a particular group of pupils.

5. Both subject matter and activities are chosen from a wide range of fields—history, geography, science, English, and the arts.

# V

## Presentation of the Data

IN PLANNING the study it was assumed that a number of factors might affect the scores which the pupils in the two counties would make upon the special spelling test given at the close of the experimental period. One of these factors, of course, would be the organization and teaching of the social studies in the two counties. This was the experimental factor being studied and the way in which it differed between the two counties has already been described. Other factors, however, which might affect the results on the final test would necessarily have to be equated; that is to say, the groups in each of the two counties would need to be approximately equal with regard to other factors which might affect the scores on the final test.

The factors which were assumed to be of importance and the tests which were used as measures of these factors are given on page 45. The factors were chronological age, intelligence score, word meaning score, literature score, reading score, history and civics score, geography score, the score on a standard spelling test, and, of course, the initial score made on the special spelling test. Data with regard to these various factors were gathered from all of the pupils participating in the experiment.[1]

Instead of attempting to equate the group representing County B with each of the three groups of County A on the basis of all of these factors, the writer attempted to equate the groups on the basis of the factors which, so far as the test data revealed, actually did affect the scores which the pupils made on the final administration of the special spelling test. The scores made in County B, which served as the control group, were correlated with

[1] These data are on file with author.

each other, giving the set of simple correlations shown in Table XI. It should be noted that the total reading score represents the combining of scores in paragraph meaning and word meaning. It was thought that the word meaning scores might have a closer relationship to the scores on Test III than the total reading score and hence these scores were treated separately as well as in combination with the scores on paragraph meaning. The two tests of social studies, the history and civics, and the geography, were combined, however, since it was not expected that either set of scores would have a closer relationship than the combined scores. In reading Table XI it should be noted that Test I represents the initial administration of the special spelling test, Test II represents the administration of the test after the first period of five weeks, and Test III represents the scores made at the end of the experimental period of fifteen weeks on the special spelling test.

Inspection of Table XI reveals a number of most interesting facts. In the first place, it is evident from the right-hand column that the total reading score is more closely related to the score on

TABLE XI

*Correlations of Various Measures of Pupils in County B (Control Group)*
*N = 151*

|  | Word Meaning | Literature | Total Reading | Social Studies | Standard Spelling | Otis Test | Spelling Test I | Spelling Test II | Spelling Test III |
|---|---|---|---|---|---|---|---|---|---|
| Age ....... | −.289 | −.208 | −.280 | −.145 | −.325 | −.238 | −.300 | −.300 | −.277 |
| Word Meaning ...... |  | .477 | .942 | .635 | .654 | .699 | .663 | .661 | .643 |
| Literature . |  |  | .540 | .515 | .368 | .493 | .434 | .445 | .430 |
| Total Reading ...... |  |  |  | .691 | .662 | .775 | .674 | .682 | .663 |
| Social Studies ...... |  |  |  |  | .385 | .688 | .455 | .467 | .448 |
| Standard Spelling .. |  |  |  |  |  | .584 | .875 | .878 | .849 |
| Otis Test .. |  |  |  |  |  |  | .582 | .580 | .577 |
| Spelling Test I ... |  |  |  |  |  |  |  | .979 | .969 |
| Spelling Test II .. |  |  |  |  |  |  |  |  | .981 |

Test III than is the score in the word meaning test. Thus, this single set of combined scores may be utilized and the word meaning scores disregarded. In the second place, it is at once apparent that the factor which is most nearly related to the final scores made by the pupils is the scores which they made upon the initial administration of the test, here labeled Test I. The correlation between Tests I and III is .969, which is extremely high. Of course Test II is even more closely related, but it represents scores made after the experiment was in progress and could not be used as a basis for equating the groups. Three other factors have relatively high correlations. These, in descending order, are: the standard spelling score, $r=.849$, the total reading score, $r=.663$, and the score on the Otis test of intelligence, $r=.577$. Significant, too, is the fact that the combined scores in the social studies are considerably lower, $r=.448$.

The factors, then, which had highest relationship to the scores pupils made upon the final administration of the spelling test in County B were the scores on Test I, the scores on the standard spelling test, the total reading scores, and the scores on the intelligence test. Equating of the groups upon the basis of these four factors should be sufficient if it can be assumed that the groups in the two counties represent similar populations with respect to other factors such as community background, competence of teachers, and the like. The choosing of the groups for just such similarities has already been noted in Chapter II.

*Relative Equality of the Groups.* The degree to which the three experimental groups in County A and the control group in County B were actually equated is shown in Tables XII to XVII. Table XII gives the means and the standard deviations of the scores of all the groups on the preliminary tests so far as the four significant factors are concerned: the first administration of the special spelling test, or Test I; the total reading score; the Otis test; and the standard spelling score. Table XIII presents similar data for chronological age, word meaning, literature, and social studies.

It has been noted above that the scores with the closest rela-

TABLE XII

*Means and Standard Deviations of Scores of All Groups on Selected Preliminary Tests*

|  |  | Group A-1 | Group A-2 | Group A-3 | Group A (Total) | Group B (Control) |
|---|---|---|---|---|---|---|
|  |  | $N = 171$ | 210 | 274 | 655 | 151 |
| Special Spelling Test | Mean ...... | 79.50 | 79.80 | 79.80 | 79.80 | 79.86 |
|  | $\sigma_M$ ......... | 3.44 | 3.04 | 2.66 | 1.74 | 3.61 |
|  | S.D. ........ | 45.00 | 44.10 | 44.10 | 44.40 | 44.28 |
|  | $\sigma_{S.D.}$ ........ | 2.43 | 2.15 | 1.88 | 1.23 | 2.55 |
| Total Reading | Mean ...... | 77.20 | 75.85 | 75.55 | 76.05 | 72.34 |
|  | $\sigma_M$ ......... | 1.00 | .84 | .80 | .50 | .99 |
|  | S.D. ........ | 13.10 | 12.15 | 13.20 | 12.85 | 12.20 |
|  | $\sigma_{S.D.}$ ........ | .71 | .59 | .56 | .36 | .70 |
| Otis Test | Mean ...... | 34.50 | 33.25 | 33.05 | 33.50 | 39.23 |
|  | $\sigma_M$ ......... | .91 | .78 | .73 | .46 | .95 |
|  | S.D. ........ | 11.90 | 11.30 | 12.15 | 11.85 | 11.71 |
|  | $\sigma_{S.D.}$ ........ | .64 | .55 | .52 | .33 | .67 |
| Standard Spelling | Mean ...... | 74.25 | 74.31 | 73.17 | 73.83 | 79.03 |
|  | $\sigma_M$ ......... | .86 | .75 | .66 | .43 | .77 |
|  | S.D. ........ | 11.22 | 10.86 | 10.86 | 10.95 | 9.39 |
|  | $\sigma_{S.D.}$ ........ | .61 | .53 | .46 | .30 | .54 |

tionship to the final achievement of the pupils were the scores on the first administration of the special spelling test. This correlation was .969. Table XII indicates that with regard to this factor the groups are practically identical both in mean scores and in standard deviations. The means vary only from 79.50 for Group A-1 to 79.86 for Group B, an inconsequential amount since the standard error of the mean of any of these groups is so much greater. Likewise, the standard deviations vary only from 44.10 in Group A-2 and Group A-3 to 45.00 in Group A-1. This difference of .90 is slight compared with the standard error of the standard deviation.

If the entire Group A is compared with Group B, the groups appear even closer to equality so far as this test reveals. The mean for Group A is 79.80 and the standard deviation is 44.40. For Group B the mean is 79.86 and the standard deviation is 44.28. Table XIX shows in terms of statistical significance the differences among the different means and the comparisons with the standard

TABLE XIII

*Means and Standard Deviations of Scores of All Groups on Additional Preliminary Tests*

| | | Group A-1 | Group A-2 | Group A-3 | Group A (Total) | Group B (Control) |
|---|---|---|---|---|---|---|
| | | N = 171 | 210 | 274 | 655 | 151 |
| Chrono-logical Age | Mean ...... | 11'11" | 11'10" | 12'00" | 11'11" | 11'10" |
| | $\sigma_M$ ......... | .79" | .62" | .70" | .41" | .67" |
| | S.D. ....... | 10.35" | 8.97" | 11.67" | 10.53" | 8.68" |
| | $\sigma_{S.D.}$ ....... | .56" | .44" | .50" | .29" | .50" |
| Word Meaning | Mean ...... | 77.27 | 75.76 | 75.44 | 76.02 | 71.54 |
| | $\sigma_M$ ......... | .91 | .81 | .75 | .47 | .89 |
| | S.D. ....... | 11.90 | 11.73 | 12.41 | 12.09 | 11.44 |
| | $\sigma_{S.D.}$ ....... | .64 | .57 | .53 | .33 | .66 |
| Litera-ture | Mean ...... | 67.97 | 66.60 | 67.70 | 67.42 | 61.80 |
| | $\sigma_M$ ......... | 1.43 | 1.42 | 1.15 | .76 | 1.50 |
| | S.D. ....... | 18.65 | 20.58 | 19.05 | 19.45 | 19.30 |
| | $\sigma_{S.D.}$ ....... | 1.01 | 1.00 | .81 | .54 | 1.11 |
| Social Studies | Mean ...... | 74.85 | 73.31 | 71.33 | 72.88 | 71.82 |
| | $\sigma_M$ ......... | 1.11 | 1.05 | .92 | .59 | 1.11 |
| | S.D. ....... | 14.52 | 15.16 | 15.20 | 15.08 | 14.26 |
| | $\sigma_{S.D.}$ ....... | .78 | .74 | .65 | .42 | .82 |

errors of the differences in means. These ratios are so small as to indicate that these differences may reasonably be attributed to chance. The formula used in computing the standard error of the difference in means was

$$\text{S.E.}_{\text{Diff. M}} = \sqrt{\sigma^2_{M_1} + \sigma^2_{M_2}}$$

on the assumption that the groups are uncorrelated. This was because equivalence had not yet been demonstrated and hence it could not be assumed that the groups were correlated. So far, then, as the most important factor affecting the final score is concerned, the groups are practically identical.

When the groups are compared with regard to the other three factors, total reading score, Otis test, and standard spelling score, however, it is evident that they are not so similar. In general the three groups in County A are alike, but they differ somewhat from the County B group.

Let us consider each of these factors separately. Table XIV is

## TABLE XIV

*Comparison of Scores of All Groups on Combined Reading Score*

| Group | No. of Cases | Means | Difference in Means | S.E.Diff. M. | Difference in Means / S.E.Diff. M. |
|---|---|---|---|---|---|
| A-1 ............ | 171 | 77.20 | | | |
| A-2 ............ | 210 | 75.85 | 1.35 | 1.31 | 1.03 |
| A-1 ............ | 171 | 77.20 | | | |
| A-3 ............ | 274 | 75.55 | 1.65 | 1.28 | 1.29 |
| A-2 ............ | 210 | 75.85 | | | |
| A-3 ............ | 274 | 75.55 | .30 | 1.16 | .26 |
| A-1 ............ | 171 | 77.20 | | | |
| B (Control) ..... | 151 | 72.34 | 4.86 | 1.41 | 3.45 |
| A-2 ............ | 210 | 75.85 | | | |
| B (Control) ..... | 151 | 72.34 | 3.51 | 1.30 | 2.70 |
| A-3 ............ | 274 | 75.55 | | | |
| B (Control) ..... | 151 | 72.34 | 3.21 | 1.27 | 2.53 |
| A (Total) ...... | 655 | 76.05 | | | |
| B (Control) ..... | 151 | 72.34 | 3.71 | 1.11 | 3.34 |

a comparison of the scores of all groups in reading. The formula used in computing the standard error of the differences in means was that for uncorrelated groups, for the reasons indicated above for the comparisons on the special spelling test. The separate comparisons among each of the three groups in County A indicate relatively small differences in means which, when divided by the standard errors of the differences in means, give ratios small enough to indicate the probability of the differences being due to chance fluctuations in the sampling. On the other hand, when each of the groups in County A is compared with the control group, there are larger differences in means in favor of County A. In Group A-1 this difference is 3.45 times its standard error, which can be interpreted to mean that the difference in means is almost certainly not due to chance. Likewise, when Group A as a whole is compared with Group B, the difference of 3.71 in means compared with the standard error of the difference gives a ratio of 3.34, which can be interpreted as meaning that the difference is almost certainly positive and not due to chance. The comparison of Group A-2 with the control group and Group A-3 with the control group give differences which, when contrasted with the standard error indicate the possibility of these differences being due to chance fluctuations.

So far as the reading scores indicate, then, there are differences in favor of the experimental groups which in the case of Group A-1 and Group A as a whole are statistically significant.

In the case of the other two equating factors, namely, the Otis test of mental ability and the standard spelling score, the observed differences are negative; that is to say, they favor the control group. The comparison with regard to the Otis test is given in Table XV. Here again the differences in means among the three

TABLE XV

*Comparison of Scores of All Groups on Otis Test*

| Group | No. of Cases | Means | Difference in Means | S.E.Diff. M. | Difference in Means / S.E.Diff. M. |
|---|---|---|---|---|---|
| A-1 ............ | 171 | 34.50 | | | |
| A-2 ............ | 210 | 33.25 | 1.25 | 1.20 | 1.04 |
| A-1 ............ | 171 | 34.50 | | | |
| A-3 ............ | 274 | 33.05 | 1.45 | 1.17 | 1.24 |
| A-2 ............ | 210 | 33.25 | | | |
| A-3 ............ | 274 | 33.05 | .20 | 1.07 | .19 |
| A-1 ............ | 171 | 34.50 | | | |
| B (Control) ..... | 151 | 39.23 | −4.73 | 1.32 | 3.58 |
| A-2 ............ | 210 | 33.25 | | | |
| B (Control)...... | 151 | 39.23 | −5.98 | 1.23 | 4.86 |
| A-3 ............ | 274 | 33.05 | | | |
| B (Control) ..... | 151 | 39.23 | −6.18 | 1.20 | 5.15 |
| A (Total) ...... | 655 | 33.50 | | | |
| B (Control) ..... | 151 | 39.23 | −5.73 | 1.05 | 5.46 |

groups in County A are small and probably due to chance. The differences between means of each of the groups in County A and the mean of the control group are in each case large enough, when compared with the standard error of the difference in means, to indicate that they do not arise from inadequacies in sampling.

It should be noted, then, that with regard to the Otis test of mental ability the groups are not equated and the differences are in favor of the control group.

Turning, then, to the standard spelling test we find a similar situation. The data are given in Table XVI. The three groups in County A have small differences among their means which, when compared with the standard errors, indicate that the differences may be due to chance. On the other hand, when each group in County A and the total group from County A is compared with the control group the difference is large, is statistically significant, and favors the control group.

These discovered differences between the groups in County A and the groups in County B are worthy of interpretation. They bear out what might be expected with regard to the two counties. On the special spelling test made up largely of new words, the children in the two counties did about equally well. But they differ on the other three factors because of differences in instructional policy and in programs of instruction.

TABLE XVI

*Comparison of Scores of All Groups on Standard Spelling Test*

| Group | No. of Cases | Means | Difference in Means | S.E.Diff. M. | Difference in Means / S.E.Diff. M. |
|---|---|---|---|---|---|
| A-1 ............ | 171 | 74.25 | | | |
| A-2 ............ | 210 | 74.31 | − .06 | 1.10 | .05 |
| A-1 ............ | 171 | 74.25 | | | |
| A-3 ............ | 274 | 73.17 | 1.08 | 1.08 | 1.00 |
| A-2 ............ | 210 | 74.31 | | | |
| A-3 ............ | 274 | 73.17 | 1.16 | 1.00 | 1.16 |
| A-1 ............ | 171 | 74.25 | | | |
| B (Control) ..... | 151 | 79.03 | −4.78 | 1.15 | 4.16 |
| A-2 ............ | 210 | 74.31 | | | |
| B (Control) ..... | 151 | 79.03 | −4.72 | 1.08 | 4.37 |
| A-3 ............ | 274 | 73.17 | | | |
| B (Control) ..... | 151 | 79.03 | −5.86 | 1.01 | 5.80 |
| A (Total)........ | 655 | 73.83 | | | |
| B (Control) ..... | 151 | 79.03 | −5.20 | .88 | 5.91 |

County A had just completed an attack on the problem of repeaters in the grades and children tended to be promoted regularly unless their achievement was unusually deficient. In County B, on the other hand, the promotion policy was much more selective and the children of less ability tended to be left behind in the lower grades. This undoubtedly accounts for the difference of 5.73 points in mean score in intelligence in the two counties. County B is a more select group and averages somewhat higher in mental ability as measured by the Otis test.

In a similar fashion the more select group in County B did somewhat better in a standard test of spelling based upon the commonest words which had been taught throughout the grades.

On the reading test, however, we find the experimental group surpassing the control group. It is reasonable to account for this in terms of the different instructional emphases in the two counties. Not only in the social studies but in general, County B tends to rely upon a limited number of textbooks as the basis of instruction. The program in County A, on the other hand, is based upon as wide reading as possible and few textbooks are used. Each classroom has its own library and children throughout the grades read many books rather than a few. In spite, then, of their somewhat inferior mental ability, these youngsters have acquired a greater average reading ability than have those in the more traditional schools of County B.

The fact that the samples from County A and from County B conform to what might be expected with regard to the results in spelling ability, reading ability, and general mental ability is evidence of the representativeness of the samples.

It may be said, then, that the three groups in County A are similar with respect to all four factors which were found to have high relationship to the final scores in the special spelling test. The control group was practically identical with the groups in County A with respect to the most important factor, the initial administration of the special spelling test. With regard to reading scores the differences between the control group and the other groups favored the experimental groups, while with regard both to the Otis test and to the standard spelling score the differences favored the control group. Since, among the four factors, the total reading score stood third with respect to the relationship to the final score, it can reasonably be held that the groups, while not identical, are similar and the differences tend to favor the control group.

The relative equality of the several groups with regard to the four factors most closely related to the success of the pupils on the final administration of the special spelling test has been indicated. It might also be of interest to determine the similarity of the groups with respect to other factors, even though these factors are not closely related to the final results. These four factors are chronological age, the score on a test of word meaning, the score on the literature test, and the combined scores representing a measure of the ability in social studies. The means and standard deviations for the several groups with regard to these factors are presented in Table XIII. This table reveals a similar pattern to that with regard to the previous four factors. The groups are quite similar in chronological age and in the test of social studies achievement. With regard to the tests on word meaning and literature the experimental groups are superior to the control group.

In chronological age the means vary from 11 years 10 months for both the control group and Group A-2 to 12 years 0 months for Group A-3. There is a difference of one month between the means of the total experimental group (M = 11 years 11 months) and the control group (M = 11 years 10 months).

In the test of the social studies the means of the groups vary from 74.85 for Group A-1 to 71.33 for Group A-3. This variation of four and a half points is not large when compared with the standard deviation, which is approximately 15 for the several groups. The mean for the total of the experimental groups is 72.88 as contrasted with the mean for the control group of 71.82, a difference of approximately one score point which is certainly not significant. In chronological age and in the test of social studies, therefore, the several groups are very similar.

The test of word meaning is one of the tests which enters into the total reading score and it shows the same characteristics shown previously by the means of the reading scores. The means of the experimental groups vary by less than two points, but the mean of the control group is several points less. The difference between the mean of the total experimental group and the mean of the control group is about four and a half score points. This difference is in favor of the experimental group.

Likewise, the means of the experimental groups are very similar on the test of literature, but the difference between the mean for the total experimental group and the mean of the control group is 5.62. Again the experimental groups exceed the control group.

These differences in favor of the experimental groups in the tests of word meaning and literature may be attributed to the program of wide reading in County A as contrasted to the more traditional textbook type of program in County B. The fact that in the preceding grades the children have read many books reveals itself in a wider acquaintance with children's literature and a somewhat larger vocabulary. On the other hand, social studies facts, found in typical courses of study and more or less traditional in nature, are known about equally well in the two counties. This equality of the groups on the social studies test is due to the fact that the test does not measure the objectives of the broad program of social studies but, instead, is based upon the facts in history, geography, and civics which appear commonly in courses of study. It is a tribute to County A that the children did as well as the pupils in County B when these facts had not been stressed as the primary objectives of the social studies in the former county.

In summary, then, the experimental groups are similar with respect to all eight factors of which measures were secured. In the initial administration of the spelling test, in social studies scores, and in chronological age the two counties were closely similar. With regard to the Otis test of mental ability and the general test of spelling ability differences favored the control group. With regard to the three tests related to reading, the test of word meaning, the total reading score, and the test of literature, the differences favored the experimental groups. Since, however, the factors of highest relationship to success on the final administration of the special spelling test were the initial scores on this test and the scores on a standard test of spelling, it is apparent that, in general, differences, though slight, favored the control group.

*Achievement of All Groups on the Special Spelling Test.* The most striking result of the experiment is that all groups gained in ability to spell the words of the special spelling test and the gains were in each case statistically significant, that is to say, they were real gains which could not reasonably be attributed to fluctuations due to the inadequacies of sampling. This was true both for the experimental period of five weeks and for the total experimental period of fifteen weeks. These data are presented in Table XVII. It will be noticed that the differences in scores between the original testing and the testing at the five-weeks period, and again the difference between the original mean scores and the means at the end of the experimental period of fifteen weeks, are each divided by its own standard error of the difference. Since the comparison is between different testings of the same group and not between uncorrelated groups, the formula which was used for determining the standard error of the differences was

$$\text{S.E.}_{\text{Diff.M.}} = \sqrt{\sigma^2_{M_1} + \sigma^2_{M_2} - 2r_{12}\sigma_{M_1}\sigma_{M_2}}.$$

The correlation which was used was, of course, the correlation between Test I and Test II, $r = .979$ for the five-week comparison, and the correlation between Test I and Test III, $r = .969$ for the fifteen-week comparison.

When the ratio of the difference divided by the standard error of the difference is 2.95 or larger, it indicates that the chances are 997 out of 1,000 that the differences would not arise from inadequacies of the sampling. When the quotients are this large or larger, it can be said that "practical certainty" exists, that the gain is not due to a sampling error. An inspection of the right-hand column of Table XVII indicates that all these ratios are very large. All the groups, the three from County A, the total group for County A, and the control group in County B, made gains of statistical significance in five weeks and much greater gains in fifteen weeks. Although the total time was three times the initial period of five weeks, the gains for the total period were not three times as great, but instead varied somewhat from group to group at a point slightly more than twice the original gain. Actually, of course, the two gains cannot be compared in this fashion since

### TABLE XVII

*Gains Made by All Groups During Experimental Period*

| Group | No. of Cases | Mean | S.E.$_M$ | S.D. | S.E.$_\sigma$ | Diff.$_M$ | S.E.$_{Diff.M}$ | Diff. Means / S.E.$_{Diff.M.}$ |
|---|---|---|---|---|---|---|---|---|
| A-1 | 171 | | | | | | | |
| Test I .... | | 79.50 | 3.44 | 45.00 | 2.43 | | | |
| Test II .... | | 93.15 | 3.80 | 49.65 | 2.69 | 13.65 | .82 | 16.65 |
| Test III .... | | 106.80 | 4.14 | 54.15 | 2.93 | 27.30 | 1.17 | 23.33 |
| A-2 | 210 | | | | | | | |
| Test I .... | | 79.80 | 3.04 | 44.10 | 2.15 | | | |
| Test II .... | | 90.30 | 3.35 | 48.60 | 2.37 | 10.50 | .72 | 14.58 |
| Test III .... | | 108.45 | 3.94 | 57.15 | 2.79 | 28.65 | 1.25 | 22.92 |
| A-3 | 274 | | | | | | | |
| Test I .... | | 79.80 | 2.66 | 44.10 | 1.88 | | | |
| Test II .... | | 91.80 | 2.95 | 48.90 | 2.09 | 12.00 | .64 | 18.75 |
| Test III .... | | 106.95 | 3.20 | 52.95 | | 27.15 | .91 | 29.84 |
| A (Total) | 655 | | | | | | | |
| Test I .... | | 79.80 | 1.74 | 44.40 | 1.23 | | | |
| Test II .... | | 91.80 | 1.92 | 49.05 | 1.36 | 12.00 | .42 | 28.57 |
| Test III .... | | 107.40 | 2.13 | 54.60 | 1.51 | 27.60 | .62 | 44.52 |
| B (Control) | 151 | | | | | | | |
| Test I .... | | 79.86 | 3.61 | 44.28 | 2.55 | | | |
| Test II .... | | 89.07 | 3.83 | 47.04 | 2.71 | 9.21 | .79 | 11.66 |
| Test III .... | | 100.14 | 4.04 | 49.69 | 2.87 | 20.28 | 1.04 | 19.50 |

there is no basis for assuming that the difficulty of learning additional words is in any sort of equal units.

It should be emphasized that this is an actual gain on the part of each of the groups and that the gain may reasonably be attributed to the social studies instruction in the two counties. All other factors but one which might conceivably be related to the gains, such as direct spelling instruction, have been equated as carefully as possible. The one possible other factor is maturation. Is it reasonable to expect that five or fifteen weeks of mental maturation might be responsible for these gains?

There is no direct evidence on this point but it should be remembered that the words tested were unusual ones occurring in the units of study but not among the common words in reading and conversation. It is doubtful if the children would have learned

TABLE

*Means and Standard Deviations of Scores*

| Group | No. of Cases | Test I | | | |
|---|---|---|---|---|---|
| | | Mean | $\sigma_M$ | S.D. | $\sigma_{S.D.}$ |
| A-1 .................... | 171 | 79.50 | 3.44 | 45.00 | 2.43 |
| A-2 .................... | 210 | 79.80 | 3.04 | 44.10 | 2.15 |
| A-3 .................... | 274 | 79.80 | 2.66 | 44.10 | 1.88 |
| A (Total) ............. | 655 | 79.80 | 1.74 | 44.40 | 1.23 |
| B (Control) ........... | 151 | 79.86 | 3.61 | 44.28 | 2.55 |

to spell any of them in the short experimental period had they not had frequent contact with them in the social studies work. As for sheer mental maturation, this is a most unlikely cause because without direct contact with the words, brightness is of aid only in making and applying generalizations with regard to study, and as previously pointed out,[2] this generalization in spelling is often a hindrance rather than a help.

*The Mean Gains of the Groups Compared.* Comparisons of the achievement of the various groups on the initial administration of the special spelling test, on the administration of the test after five weeks, and the test results after fifteen weeks are given in Tables XVIII to XXI. A summary of the three testings without numerical comparisons is given in Table XVIII. It can be seen, as has been indicated earlier, that the results from all the groups were practically identical on the initial testing. Neither the means nor the standard deviations varied significantly. Comparison of the means of the groups in the initial testing are given in Table XIX. It can readily be seen that the differences are slight and without statistical significance.

One conclusion from these scores on the initial administration of the spelling test should not be overlooked. The mean score of all the groups indicated that the boys and girls in all these groups could spell an average of 79 words of the 260 upon which they

[2] Herbert Allen Carroll, *Generalization of Bright·and Dull Children: A Comparative Study with Special Reference to Spelling.* Bureau of Publications, Teachers College, Columbia University, New York, 1930.

XVIII

*of All Groups on Tests I, II, and III*

| | Test II | | | | Test III | | |
|---|---|---|---|---|---|---|---|
| Mean | $\sigma_M$ | S.D. | $\sigma_{S.D.}$ | Mean | $\sigma_M$ | S.D. | $\sigma_{S.D.}$ |
| 93.15 | 3.80 | 49.65 | 2.69 | 106.80 | 4.14 | 54.15 | 2.93 |
| 90.30 | 3.35 | 48.60 | 2.37 | 108.45 | 3.94 | 57.15 | 2.79 |
| 91.80 | 2.95 | 48.90 | 2.09 | 106.95 | 3.20 | 52.95 | 2.26 |
| 91.80 | 1.92 | 49.05 | 1.36 | 107.40 | 2.13 | 54.60 | 1.51 |
| 89.07 | 3.83 | 47.04 | 2.71 | 100.14 | 4.04 | 49.69 | 2.87 |

were tested and upon which they had never had formal instruction. In other words, on the average, the children had acquired incidentally the ability to spell over 30 per cent of the words before the study began. Since all the 260 words upon which they were tested are outside of the 3,000 commonest words and their spelling instruction had been based upon the common words, this preliminary testing indicates the fact of incidental learning. It should be noted, too, that the figure of 79 represents an average. Some of the children scored very high on the initial testing, spelling correctly more than 250 out of the 260 words. Others, of course, made scores approaching zero.

After five weeks (see "Test II" in the table) variations among the groups in average achievement began to appear. Group A-1 has the highest mean, 93.15, while the control group has the lowest mean of 89.07. The second highest is Group A-3 with a mean score of 91.80. This same score also proves to be the score for Group A taken as a whole. Group A-2, with a mean of 90.30, is the lowest of the experimental groups, although it is still higher than the control group, 89.07. After five weeks, then, all the experimental groups made scores greater than the control group and they varied to a considerable degree among themselves.

If one wants to generalize about these gains in terms of their universality, one should examine Table XX. In this table the gains are compared with the standard errors of the differences in means and this gives an indication of whether such gains may be expected under similar conditions with similar groups. Only

## TABLE XIX

*Comparison of Scores of All Groups on Spelling Test I (Initial Administration of Special Spelling Test)*

| Group | No. of Cases | Mean | Difference in Means | S.E.Diff. M. | Difference in Means / S.E.Diff. M. |
|---|---|---|---|---|---|
| A-1 ............ | 171 | 79.50 | | | |
| A-2 ............ | 210 | 79.80 | − .30 | 4.59 | .07 |
| A-1 ............ | 171 | 79.50 | | | |
| A-3 ............ | 274 | 79.80 | − .03 | 4.35 | .01 |
| A-2 ............ | 210 | 79.80 | | | |
| A-3 ............ | 274 | 79.80 | .00 | 4.04 | .00 |
| A-1 ............ | 171 | 79.50 | | | |
| B (Control) ..... | 151 | 79.86 | − .36 | 4.99 | .07 |
| A-2 ............ | 210 | 79.80 | | | |
| B (Control) ..... | 151 | 79.86 | − .06 | 4.72 | .01 |
| A-3 ............ | 274 | 79.80 | | | |
| B (Control) ..... | 151 | 79.86 | − .06 | 4.48 | .01 |
| A (Total) ...... | 655 | 79.80 | | | |
| B (Control) ..... | 151 | 79.86 | − .06 | 4.01 | .01 |

when the ratio of the difference in means divided by the standard error of the difference in means is equal to 2.95 or larger can it be said with practical certainty that these results may be expected under similar conditions with other groups. It will be noted that in only one case is the ratio this large, and that is when Group A-1 is compared with the control group. It is reasonable to conclude, then, that while in this experiment five weeks of the study brought differences in achievement on the special spelling test, these differences were in only one case large enough to justify more universal application of the conclusion. In all cases in which an experimental group is compared with the control group the chances are relatively high that there is a difference in favor of the experimental group but relative certainty is not attained.

After fifteen weeks of the experiment, however, the results were much more conclusive. An examination of Table XVIII indicates that the mean achievement of the experimental groups becomes more nearly alike, for the greatest variation is only 1.65. This

## TABLE XX

*Comparison of Scores of All Groups on Spelling Test II (Special Spelling Test Administered After Five-Week Experimental Period)*

| Group | No. of Cases | Mean | Difference in Means | S.E.Diff. M. | Difference in Means S.E.Diff. M. |
|---|---|---|---|---|---|
| A-1 ............ | 171 | 93.15 | | | |
| A-2 ............ | 210 | 90.30 | 2.85 | .86 | 3.31 |
| A-1 ............ | 171 | 93.15 | | | |
| A-3 ............ | 274 | 91.80 | 1.35 | 1.09 | 1.24 |
| A-2 ............ | 210 | 90.30 | | | |
| A-3 ............ | 274 | 91.80 | −1.50 | .76 | 1.97 |
| A-1 ............ | 171 | 93.15 | | | |
| B (Control) ..... | 151 | 89.07 | 4.08 | .78 | 5.23 |
| A-2 ............ | 210 | 90.30 | | | |
| B (Control) ..... | 151 | 89.07 | 1.23 | .88 | 1.40 |
| A-3 ............ | 274 | 91.80 | | | |
| B (Control) ..... | 151 | 89.07 | 2.73 | 1.12 | 2.44 |
| A (Total) ...... | 655 | 91.80 | | | |
| B (Control)...... | 151 | 89.07 | 2.73 | 1.99 | 1.37 |

can be explained by the fact that these three similar groups had now had, in general, the same instruction, for each had spent the fifteen weeks covering the same three units in the course of study. On the other hand, the disparities between the experimental groups and the control group are larger, the differences varying from 6.66 between Group A-1 and the control group and 8.31 between Group A-2 and the control group. Table XXI shows that the differences between each of the experimental groups and the control group and between the experimental group as a whole and the control group are great enough to be statistically significant. This permits the application of these findings to a more general population. It can be said, then, that similar groups of pupils under similar conditions can be expected to achieve more in their spelling of these experimental words when taught under the conditions of County A than they could under the conditions of County B provided that the period of the experiment is at least as long as fifteen weeks, as it was in this study.

*Comparison of the Groups by Prediction.* The previous section presented a comparison of the various groups on the basis of group means. This method is reliable when groups are comparable and it has been shown that, for the purposes of this study, the groups

TABLE XXI

*Comparison of Scores of All Groups on Spelling Test III (Special Spelling Test Administered After Fifteen-Week Experimental Period)*

| Group | No. of Cases | Mean | Difference in Means | S.E.Diff. M | Difference in Means / S.E.Diff. M. |
|---|---|---|---|---|---|
| A-1 ............. | 171 | 106.80 | | | |
| A-2 ............. | 210 | 108.45 | −1.65 | 1.03 | 1.60 |
| A-1 ............ | 171 | 106.80 | | | |
| A-3 ............ | 274 | 106.95 | − .15 | 1.31 | .11 |
| A-2 ............ | 210 | 108.45 | | | |
| A-3 ............ | 274 | 106.95 | 1.50 | 1.15 | 1.30 |
| A-1 ............ | 171 | 106.80 | | | |
| B (Control) ..... | 151 | 100.14 | 6.66 | 1.02 | 6.53 |
| A-2 ............ | 210 | 108.45 | | | |
| B (Control) ..... | 151 | 100.14 | 8.31 | 1.00 | 8.31 |
| A-3 ............ | 274 | 106.95 | | | |
| B (Control) ..... | 151 | 100.14 | 6.81 | 1.23 | 5.54 |
| A (Total) ...... | 655 | 107.40 | | | |
| B (Control) ..... | 151 | 100.14 | 7.26 | 2.05 | 3.54 |

were similar enough to permit such comparisons. However, as a check upon these findings another method of comparison was used which does not require such close similarity among the groups being compared. This method is based upon the use of prediction by means of a regression equation. In the method of prediction we develop a regression equation on the basis of the factors which seem to have highest relationship to our success criterion so far as the control group is concerned. By identifying the factors with high relationship to success in the control group, one is able to determine what the factors are which influence success. The regression equation gives a mathematical statement of the relative influence of each of the factors upon success. This regression equation, based upon the control group, can then be utilized to predict what a pupil in the experimental group would have achieved had he been in the control group. Comparing his actual achievement with his predicted achievement gives a measure of the effect of the experimental factor.

Of course, an individual score might vary somewhat from the predicted score because of chance fluctuations, but when predictions are worked out for a group of pupils and these are compared with the actual scores, the differences are reliable indications of the effect of the experimental factor.

In developing a regression equation attention was first paid to the various elements with highest relationship to the success criterion. This success criterion, of course, was the score made on the final testing of the group with the special spelling test. The relation of the various factors to this final score, or Test III, is given in Table XI. Ignoring the relationship between Test II and Test III, since Test II had not been given at the beginning of the experiment, it becomes evident that the factors with highest relationship are: (1) the score on Test I, $r = .969$ (actually .9686); (2) the score on the standard spelling test, $r = .849$; (3) the total reading score, $r = .663$; and (4) the score on the Otis Test of Mental Ability, $r = .577$. The multiple correlation among these four factors was $R_{(1)2345} = .9688$. The formula used in this computation was as follows:

$$R_{(1)2345} = \sqrt{1 - (1 - r_{12}{}^2)(1 - r_{13 \cdot 2}{}^2)(1 - r_{14 \cdot 23}{}^2)(1 - r_{15 \cdot 234}{}^2)}$$

Substituting the indicated values:

$$R_{(1)2345} = \sqrt{1 - (1 - .6628^2)(1 - .7311^2)(1 - .0372^2)(1 - .8741^2)}$$

where 1 equals Test III score, 2 equals reading score, 3 equals standard spelling score, 4 equals Otis test score, and 5 equals score on Test I.

From this multiple correlation it is possible to develop a regression equation with five variables which could be used for prediction as indicated above. This formula was developed and is as follows:

$$Y_1 = .0266X_2 - .0158X_3 + .1140X_4 + 1.073X_5 + 9.303$$

Before going to the tremendous labor of computing the 655

scores by means of this formula, a comparison was made between its value, involving as it does four factors of prediction, and the simple correlation between Test III and Test I. Usually the addition of more factors to a regression equation adds considerably to its accuracy, but in this case the simple correlation between Test I and Test III was so high that the multiple correlation proved to add little to the accuracy of prediction. The two correlations were:

$$r_{15} = .9686$$
$$R_{(1)2345} = .9688$$

Thus, the addition of the three factors only contributes .0002 to the accuracy of the prediction.

Further to safeguard this fact before substituting a regression equation based on the simple correlation for the more complex regression equation above, the investigator computed on the two bases the scores of twenty-five pupils selected at random. The results are presented in Table XXII. Inspection of this table will indicate that the means of the two sets of calculated scores are approximately equal and that in thirteen of the twenty-five cases scores in one set are higher and in twelve of the twenty-five cases scores in the other set are higher. It is fairly certain, then, that when used with a group the short regression equation based upon the simple correlation between Test I and Test III will give as satisfactory results as the more complex equation.

The regression equation using the simple correlation between the initial test and the final test, $r = .9686$, was:

$$Y = 1.08X + 13.51$$

Using this simple regression equation, scores were predicted for the 655 cases in the experimental group. These scores were then distributed and the means and standard deviations computed. The predicted scores of the various experimental groups compared with their actual scores are given in Table XXIII. This table is to be interpreted as meaning that had the pupils in the experimental group been members of the control group they would have made the predicted scores. The fact that their actual scores are higher, then, is to be attributed to their membership in the experimental groups. The experimental factor in the experimental groups has been

## TABLE XXII

*Comparison of Scores Predicted on Basis of Regression Equation with Five Variables and Those Predicted on the Basis of Regression Equation with Two Variables for 25 Cases Selected at Random*

| Pupil | Scores | |
|---|---|---|
| | Five Variables | Two Variables |
| 1 ................. | 155.95 | 154.99 |
| 2 ................. | 220.82 | 219.79 |
| 3 ................. | 211.97 | 212.23 |
| 4 ................. | 33.77 | 36.19 |
| 5 ................. | 19.28 | 18.91 |
| 6 ................. | 33.42 | 34.03 |
| 7 ................. | 23.29 | 23.23 |
| 8 ................. | 21.54 | 23.23 |
| 9 ................. | 17.63 | 19.99 |
| 10 ................. | 31.14 | 31.87 |
| 11 ................. | 70.96 | 73.99 |
| 12 ................. | 143.30 | 146.35 |
| 13 ................. | 225.42 | 224.11 |
| 14 ................. | 218.51 | 217.63 |
| 15 ................. | 110.86 | 112.87 |
| 16 ................. | 190.82 | 189.53 |
| 17 ................. | 71.88 | 72.91 |
| 18 ................. | 278.04 | 275.95 |
| 19 ................. | 170.88 | 169.03 |
| 20 ................. | 123.42 | 122.59 |
| 21 ................. | 127.21 | 125.83 |
| 22 ................. | 123.07 | 122.59 |
| 23 ................. | 79.80 | 80.47 |
| 24 ................. | 134.12 | 132.31 |
| 25 ................. | 74.59 | 75.07 |
| Mean ............. | 116.47 | 116.63 |

Note: In 13 cases scores computed with five variables are higher; in 12 cases scores computed with two variables are higher.

identified as the total organization and plan of teaching of the social studies in County A as contrasted with County B. The differences in the means between the actual and the predicted scores, then, become a measure of the effectiveness of the experimental factor.

It should be noted in Table XXIII that each group actually made scores considerably higher than was predicted and that the differences in means when divided by the standard error of these differences give ratios ranging from 6.97 to 15.00. Thus the differences

### TABLE XXIII

*Comparison of Actual and Predicted Scores on Special Spelling Test Given at Close of Fifteen-Week Experimental Period. Prediction Based on Regression Equation from 151 Cases in Control Group*

| Group | No. of Cases | Mean | S.E.$_M$ | S.D. | S.E.$_\sigma$ | Difference in Means | S.E.$_{Diff.M}$ | $\frac{Diff.Means}{S.E._{Diff.M}}$ |
|---|---|---|---|---|---|---|---|---|
| A-1 (Actual) .. | 171 | 106.80 | 4.14 | 54.15 | 2.93 | | | |
| A-1 (Predicted) | 171 | 98.85 | 3.51 | 45.90 | 2.48 | 7.95 | 1.14 | 6.97 |
| A-2 (Actual) .. | 210 | 108.45 | 3.94 | 57.15 | 2.79 | | | |
| A-2 (Predicted) | 210 | 99.00 | 3.28 | 47.55 | 2.32 | 9.45 | 1.11 | 8.51 |
| A-3 (Actual) .. | 274 | 106.95 | 3.20 | 52.95 | 2.26 | | | |
| A-3 (Predicted) | 274 | 99.00 | 2.88 | 47.70 | 2.04 | 7.95 | .82 | 9.70 |
| Total A (Actual) .... | 655 | 107.40 | 2.13 | 54.60 | 1.51 | | | |
| Total A (Predicted) . | 655 | 99.00 | 1.86 | 47.70 | 1.32 | 8.40 | .56 | 15.00 |

are in every case significant and conclusions can be made upon the basis of these findings with assurance of their reliability. Without question, the pupils in County A achieved more in their spelling of these special words than did the pupils in County B and this may safely be attributed to the definite methods of organizing and teaching the social studies in the two counties. The unit approach produced greater gains in secondary learning of spelling than did the more traditional type of teaching.

*Comparison of Gains of High and Low Groups.* While it is clear from the preceding section that pupils taken as a group tended to gain more in the experimental situation, it is still important to discover whether these gains are made rather uniformly by all pupils or whether they are made by average and bright pupils alone or, perhaps, by pupils at the lower end of the distribution.

In order to answer this question the entire group of pupils in County A was taken as a whole and the highest and lowest fifths separated out for purposes of special study. These high and low fifths were taken separately on the basis of various abilities. First, the highest fifth on the mental test and the lowest fifth on the mental test were separated from the group and their scores recorded and tabulations made. These cases were then restored to the group and the highest fifth in reading and the lowest fifth in reading were separated and tabulated. Similarly the highest and lowest fifths in the standard spelling scores and in the initial administration of the special spelling test were separated and tabulated.

The simplest way of comparing these pupils of high and low ability is to count the number and percentage of them who exceeded their prediction. This percentage can then be compared with the percentage among a similar group in the control group. It should be pointed out at this point that in the entire control group as many might be expected to exceed the predicted score slightly as to fall below it slightly since the prediction was based upon the actual results in the control group. However, if one takes the upper or lower fifth of the control group, this would not necessarily be true since the predictions are on the basis of the total distribution and the extremes of the distribution may be somewhat skewed. For accuracy, then, one should count the number who exceed and fall below prediction in each of the fifths of the control group just as one did with the experimental group. The number and percentage for the highest fifth selected on the various bases of the experimental groups are presented in Table XXIV and similar data for the highest fifth in the control group are presented in Table XXV. To interpret these data the two tables should be compared.

For a pupil in the highest fifth in mental ability the chances are nearly four to one of exceeding the predicted achievement in secondary learning of spelling if he is located in the experimental group. If he is in the control group, however, his chances of doing better than the average of the control group are only $1\frac{1}{2}$ to 1. It is safe to conclude from this that the bright pupils benefit greatly from being taught under the experimental conditions in County A.

TABLE XXIV

*Number and Percentage of Pupils in Highest Fifth of Group A (Total Experimental Group) Selected on Basis of Otis Test Scores, Reading Scores, Standard Spelling Scores and Special Spelling Test, Who Exceeded or Fell Below Scores Predicted on Basis of Achievement in Control Group. N = 131*

| Highest Fifth In: | Exceeded Prediction | | Fell Below Prediction | |
|---|---|---|---|---|
| | Number | Per Cent | Number | Per Cent |
| Otis Test Scores ............. | 104 | 79.4 | 27 | 20.6 |
| Reading Scores .............. | 101 | 77.1 | 30 | 22.9 |
| Standard Spelling Score ...... | 103 | 78.6 | 28 | 21.4 |
| Special Spelling Test ......... | 104 | 79.4 | 27 | 20.6 |

For a pupil in the upper fifth of his group in reading ability the chances are about 3½ to 1 of exceeding prediction if he is located in the experimental group. If he is a member of the control group, however, his chances of exceeding the average of the control group are again only 1½ to 1. Again, one may conclude that

TABLE XXV

*Number and Percentage of Pupils in Highest Fifth of Group B (Control Group) Selected on Basis of Otis Test Scores, Reading Scores, Standard Spelling Scores and Special Spelling Test, Who Exceeded or Fell Below Scores Predicted on Basis of Achievement of Total Group B. N = 30*

| Highest Fifth In: | Exceeded Prediction | | Fell Below Prediction | |
|---|---|---|---|---|
| | Number | Per Cent | Number | Per Cent |
| Otis Test Scores ............. | 18 | 60.0 | 12 | 40.0 |
| Reading Scores .............. | 18 | 60.0 | 12 | 40.0 |
| Standard Spelling Scores ..... | 17 | 56.7 | 13 | 43.3 |
| Special Spelling Test ......... | 17 | 56.7 | 13 | 43.3 |

pupils in the upper fifth of the group in reading ability as in mental ability benefit much more in secondary learning in the experimental county than they do under the more traditional conditions in County B.

The highest fifth in general spelling ability and the highest fifth in the performance on the special spelling test have even greater chances for achievement in secondary learning of spelling under the experimental conditions than they did under the conditions of the control group. The chances of exceeding prediction are from 3½ to 1 to nearly 4 to 1 among these pupils in the experimental group, whereas the chances of exceeding prediction in the control group are only slightly better than even.

In a similar fashion the achievement of pupils in the lowest fifth of the experimental group and in the lowest fifth of the control group can be compared. These data are given in Tables XXVI and

TABLE XXVI

*Number and Percentage of Pupils in Lowest Fifth of Total Experimental Group
Selected on Basis of Otis Test Scores, Reading Scores, Standard
Spelling Scores and Special Spelling Test Scores, Who
Exceeded or Fell Below Scores Predicted on Basis of
Achievement in Control Group. N = 131*

| Lowest Fifth In: | Exceeded Prediction | | Fell Below Prediction | |
|---|---|---|---|---|
| | Number | Per Cent | Number | Per Cent |
| Otis Test Scores ............ | 63 | 48.1 | 68 | 51.9 |
| Reading Scores .............. | 51 | 38.9 | 80 | 61.1 |
| Standard Spelling Score ...... | 45 | 34.4 | 86 | 65.6 |
| Special Spelling Test ......... | 47 | 35.9 | 84 | 64.1 |

XXVII. Let us look first at the pupils in the lowest fifth in mental ability. This lowest fifth in the experimental group achieved about the same as the average pupil in the control group. That is, the chances of a pupil in the lowest fifth in intelligence of exceeding the prediction are about even. In fact, they are slightly less than even, but the chances are still greater than they are for a similar pupil in the lowest fifth in intelligence in the control group. He has only one chance in three of exceeding the predicted score. That is to say, the chances are 2 to 1 against him. We can conclude, then, that even pupils in the lowest fifth in mental ability still benefit more from the experimental conditions than they do from the conditions in the control group.

A different picture is presented by the pupils representing the

TABLE XXVII

*Number and Percentage of Pupils in Lowest Fifth of Group B (Control Group)*
*Selected on Basis of Otis Test Scores, Reading Scores, Standard*
*Spelling Scores and Special Spelling Test, Who Exceeded or*
*Fell Below Scores Predicted on Basis of Achievement*
*of Total Group B. N = 30*

| Lowest Fifth In: | Exceeded Prediction | | Fell Below Prediction | |
|---|---|---|---|---|
| | Number | Per Cent | Number | Per Cent |
| Otis Test Scores ............. | 10 | 33.3 | 20 | 66.7 |
| Reading Scores .............. | 15 | 50.0 | 15 | 50.0 |
| Standard Spelling Scores ..... | 10 | 33.3 | 20 | 66.7 |
| Special Spelling Test ......... | 10 | 33.3 | 20 | 66.7 |

lowest fifth in reading ability. In this case the poorer readers benefit more in secondary learning of spelling from being taught their social studies by traditional methods than they do under the experimental conditions. In the control group their chances are even of exceeding the prediction, but in the experimental group the chances are about $1\frac{2}{3}$ to 1 against them.

Looking next at the pupils in the lowest fifth in general spelling ability one discovers that it makes little difference whether these pupils are located in the experimental group or in the control group. In both cases the chances are about 2 to 1 against their exceeding prediction. Almost exactly the same situation exists for the pupils in the lowest fifth on the special spelling test. Chances are about the same in the two groups, in each case being about 2 to 1 against the pupil exceeding the prediction.

A direct comparison of the means of the upper and lower fifths of the total experimental group and the control group affords a second method of determining where the gains are made. The data for the upper fifths of the groups selected on various bases is given in Table XXVIII. It will be noted that the differences of the means between the experimental group and the control group vary from 10.35 points for the highest fifth in general spelling ability to 26.00 points for the highest fifth of the group on the special spelling test, and all of the differences are statistically sig-

TABLE XXVIII

*Comparison of Means of Highest Fifth of Pupils in Various Abilities in the Control and Experimental Groups*

| Highest Fifth In: | No. of Cases | Mean | S. E.$_M$ | S. D. | S. E.$_\sigma$ | Difference in Means | S. E.$_{Diff. M}$ | Difference in Means S. E.$_{Diff. M}$ |
|---|---|---|---|---|---|---|---|---|
| Otis Test | | | | | | | | |
| Experimental ...... | 131 | 160.65 | 3.93 | 44.96 | 2.78 | 19.05 | 4.23 | 4.50 |
| Control .......... | 30 | 141.60 | 7.93 | 43.44 | 5.61 | | | |
| Reading Test | | | | | | | | |
| Experimental ...... | 131 | 160.05 | 3.98 | 45.60 | 2.82 | 13.65 | 2.29 | 5.96 |
| Control .......... | 30 | 146.40 | 5.93 | 40.92 | 5.28 | | | |
| Standard Spelling Test | | | | | | | | |
| Experimental ...... | 131 | 175.95 | 2.99 | 34.20 | 2.11 | 10.35 | 2.17 | 4.77 |
| Control .......... | 30 | 165.60 | 4.94 | 27.06 | 3.49 | | | |
| Special Spelling Test | | | | | | | | |
| Experimental ...... | 131 | 185.40 | 2.41 | 27.60 | 1.70 | 26.00 | 1.61 | 16.15 |
| Control .......... | 30 | 159.40 | 3.83 | 21.00 | 2.71 | | | |

nificant. Compare these differences with that between the means of the entire experimental group and the entire control group, which is 7.26 points (see Table XXI), and it can readily be seen that those in the upper fifth gain much more proportionately. The upper fifth in general spelling ability gain slightly over three points more than the average pupil but those in the upper fifth in reading gain considerably more. Those pupils who are high in mental ability and those who did best on the initial administration of the special spelling test gained from two and one-half times to over three times more than the average pupil. The abler pupils, then, profit much more from the experimental conditions than do the average pupils.

For the comparison of the means of the lowest fifths of the control and experimental groups, Table XXIX should be examined. The differences in means vary from 1.25 to 8.85 as compared with the difference in means for the total groups of 7.26. The smallest difference has such a large standard error as to indicate the probability of its being due to chance. The other differences are all statistically significant, however. What do these differences indicate? In the case of the lower fifth in mental ability the difference indicates not only that these children in the experi-

### TABLE XXIX

*Comparison of Means of Lowest Fifth of Pupils in Various Abilities in the Control and Experimental Groups*

| Highest Fifth In: | No. of Cases | Mean | S. E.$_M$ | S. D. | S. E.$_\sigma$ | Difference in Means | S. E.$_{Diff.M}$ | Difference in Means / S. E.$_{Diff.M}$ |
|---|---|---|---|---|---|---|---|---|
| **Otis Test** | | | | | | | | |
| Experimental ...... | 131 | 58.05 | 2.96 | 33.90 | 2.09 | 1.25 | 3.75 | .33 |
| Control .......... | 30 | 56.80 | 6.55 | 35.88 | 4.63 | | | |
| **Reading Test** | | | | | | | | |
| Experimental ...... | 131 | 56.25 | 3.42 | 39.15 | 2.42 | 5.25 | 1.56 | 3.37 |
| Control .......... | 30 | 51.00 | 4.81 | 26.94 | 3.48 | | | |
| **Standard Spelling Test** | | | | | | | | |
| Experimental ...... | 131 | 46.65 | 2.50 | 28.65 | 1.77 | 8.85 | .79 | 11.20 |
| Control .......... | 30 | 37.80 | 2.92 | 16.02 | 2.07 | | | |
| **Special Spelling Test** | | | | | | | | |
| Experimental ...... | 131 | 40.35 | 1.62 | 18.60 | 1.15 | 5.75 | .44 | 13.07 |
| Control .......... | 30 | 34.60 | 1.39 | 7.59 | .98 | | | |

mental group do not gain as much as the average of the experimental group, but that they gain little if any more than did children of similar ability in the control group. For the lowest fifths in reading, general spelling ability, and Test I, the differences indicate an advantage for the experimental group approaching or exceeding the general advantage of the entire experimental group.

A third way of comparing the incidental learning of spelling of students of high and low ability is to compare the means of the actual scores made by the upper and lower fifths with the means of the predicted scores. This method is the same as that used in comparing the actual and predicted scores for the whole of the experimental groups.

In applying this technique the data described above were used; that is, the highest and lowest fifths respectively on the Otis test of mental ability, the highest and lowest fifths in reading ability, the highest and lowest fifths in general spelling ability, and the highest and lowest fifths on the initial administration of the special spelling test were selected. These scores were then distributed and means and standard deviations were computed. The differences in the means of the actual scores and those predicted on the basis of the regression equation could then be compared with the

## TABLE XXX

*Comparison of Actual and Predicted Scores on Special Spelling Test Given at Close of Fifteen-Week Experimental Period for Pupils in Highest Fifth of Total Experimental Group Selected on Basis of Otis Test Scores, Reading Scores, Standard Spelling Scores and Special Spelling Test Scores. Prediction Based on Regression Equation from 151 Cases in Control Group*

| Highest Fifth In: | No. of Cases | Mean | S. E.$_M$ | S. D. | S. E.$_\sigma$ | Difference in Means | S. E.$_{Diff. M}$ | Difference in Means / S. E.$_{Diff. M}$ |
|---|---|---|---|---|---|---|---|---|
| **Otis Test** | | | | | | | | |
| Actual | 131 | 160.65 | 3.93 | 44.96 | 2.78 | | | |
| Predicted | 131 | 148.20 | 3.79 | 43.35 | 2.68 | 12.45 | .97 | 12.84 |
| **Reading Test** | | | | | | | | |
| Actual | 131 | 160.05 | 3.98 | 45.60 | 2.82 | | | |
| Predicted | 131 | 148.50 | 3.79 | 43.35 | 2.68 | 11.55 | .99 | 11.67 |
| **Standard Spelling Test** | | | | | | | | |
| Actual | 131 | 175.95 | 2.99 | 34.20 | 2.11 | | | |
| Predicted | 131 | 165.45 | 2.92 | 33.45 | 2.07 | 10.50 | .74 | 14.19 |
| **Special Spelling Test** | | | | | | | | |
| Actual | 131 | 185.40 | 2.41 | 27.60 | 1.70 | | | |
| Predicted | 131 | 172.95 | 2.20 | 25.20 | 1.56 | 12.45 | .61 | 20.41 |

standard error of the difference in means. The results are given in Tables XXX and XXXI.

Let us examine first Table XXX and compare the highest fifths on the various bases. The first conclusion to be drawn from this table is that the differences in the means of the actual scores and the predicted scores are greater for this high group than for the total group. This can be seen by comparing Table XXX with Table XXIII. The difference in means of the predicted scores of the total experimental group and the actual scores of this group is 8.40. For the highest fifth the difference in means varies from 12.45 for the highest fifth in intelligence and in the special spelling test to 10.50 for the highest fifth in general spelling ability. From this we can conclude that the brighter children gain more from the experimental conditions than do the average members of the group. That this conclusion has some universality is indicated by the fact that all of the ratios obtained by dividing the differences of the means by the standard errors of the differences in means

### TABLE XXXI

*Comparison of Actual and Predicted Scores on Special Spelling Test Given at Close of Fifteen-Week Experimental Period for Pupils in Lowest Fifth of Total Experimental Group Selected on Basis of Otis Test Scores, Reading Scores, Standard Spelling Scores and Special Spelling Test Scores. Prediction Based on Regression Equation from 151 Cases in Control Group*

| Lowest Fifth In: | No. of Cases | Mean | S. E.$_M$ | S. D. | S. E.$_\sigma$ | Difference in Means | S. E.$_{Diff. M}$ | Difference in Means / S. E.$_{Diff. M}$ |
|---|---|---|---|---|---|---|---|---|
| **Otis Test** | | | | | | | | |
| Actual ............ | 131 | 58.05 | 2.96 | 33.90 | 2.09 | | | |
| Predicted ......... | 131 | 55.20 | 2.25 | 25.80 | 1.59 | 2.85 | .93 | 3.06 |
| **Reading Test** | | | | | | | | |
| Actual ............ | 131 | 56.25 | 3.42 | 39.15 | 2.42 | | | |
| Predicted ......... | 131 | 54.90 | 2.49 | 28.50 | 1.76 | 1.35 | 1.18 | 1.14 |
| **Standard Spelling Test** | | | | | | | | |
| Actual ............ | 131 | 46.65 | 2.50 | 28.65 | 1.77 | | | |
| Predicted ......... | 131 | 47.25 | 1.86 | 21.30 | 1.32 | −.60 | .84 | .71 |
| **Special Spelling Test** | | | | | | | | |
| Actual ............ | 131 | 40.35 | 1.62 | 18.60 | 1.15 | | | |
| Predicted ......... | 131 | 40.35 | .98 | 11.25 | .69 | .00 | .71 | .00 |

are so great as to leave no doubt of the statistical significance of the differences.

Table XXX also should be compared with similar data for the control group given in Table XXXII. In this table the actual and predicted scores are compared for the control group. It might be expected that the means would be identical for the predicted and the actual scores in the control group since the regression equation is based on this group. This is true for the distribution of the total group, but because the curve is somewhat skewed it does not prove true for the ends of the distribution. However, the actual and predicted means of the control group for the upper fifth of the pupils vary but slightly except in the case of the upper fifth in scores on the special spelling test. Here the difference is 2.40 in favor of the predicted scores, but this difference is not great enough to be statistically significant. The fact that the differences in the means of the actual scores and the predicted scores for the upper fifths of the experimental groups, as shown in Table XXX, are so much greater and are certainly not due to chance is evidence of the advantage of the experimental conditions over the control conditions for the children of high ability of the various types.

In a similar fashion the lowest fifths on the various bases can be compared with the total group. Table XXXI gives the means and standard deviations of the actual scores and the predicted scores of the lowest fifth of the group in mental ability, in reading ability, in general spelling ability, and on the initial administration of the special spelling test. Here again the differences in means can be compared with the differences in means of the total group as given in Table XXIII. Where the difference in means between the actual scores and the predicted scores of the total group is 8.40, the differences for the lowest fifth range from only 2.85 to —.60. We can conclude immediately that most of the gains of the experimental group are not made by the group which is low in the various abilities. Indeed, the only difference in means which has statistical significance is the difference of 2.85 made by the lowest fifth in mental ability. This difference favors the experimental group, and the ratio of this difference to its own standard error is 3.06. We can assert, then, that the lowest fifth in mental ability still gains more in the experimental group than in the control group, though the amount gained is not nearly as great as for the student of average ability. This confirms the previous conclusion which was made on the basis of the percentage of these pupils who exceeded their prediction in the experimental group as contrasted with a similar percentage in the control group. The other differences ranging from 1.35 to —.60 are so small, when compared with their own standard errors, as to indicate that they may reasonably be attributed to chance. For the lowest fifth in reading ability, in general spelling ability, and on the initial administration of the special spelling test this method demonstrated no advantage for those in the experimental group.

A comparison of the results for the lowest fifth of the experimental group, Table XXXI, and the lowest fifth of the control group, Table XXXIII, is also of interest. It is evident that the advantage of the experimental conditions for the lowest group becomes more probable. In the control group such youngsters

## TABLE XXXII

*Comparison of Actual and Predicted Scores on Special Spelling Test Given at Close of Fifteen-Week Experimental Period for Pupils in Highest Fifth of Control Group. Prediction Based on Regression Equation from Whole of Control Group*

| Highest Fifth | No. of Cases | Mean | S. E.ᴍ | S. D. | S. E.σ | Difference in Means | S. E.Diff. M | Difference in Means / S. E.Diff. M |
|---|---|---|---|---|---|---|---|---|
| **Otis Test** | | | | | | | | |
| Actual ........... | 30 | 141.60 | 7.93 | 43.44 | 5.61 | .80 | 1.99 | .40 |
| Predicted ........ | 30 | 140.80 | 8.06 | 44.16 | 5.70 | | | |
| **Reading Test** | | | | | | | | |
| Actual ........... | 30 | 146.40 | 5.93 | 40.92 | 5.28 | −.40 | 2.15 | .19 |
| Predicted ........ | 30 | 146.80 | 7.32 | 40.08 | 5.18 | | | |
| **Standard Spelling Test** | | | | | | | | |
| Actual ........... | 30 | 165.60 | 4.94 | 27.06 | 3.49 | .20 | 1.34 | .15 |
| Predicted ........ | 30 | 165.40 | 5.34 | 29.28 | 3.76 | | | |
| **Special Spelling Test** | | | | | | | | |
| Actual ........... | 30 | 159.40 | 3.83 | 21.00 | 2.71 | −2.40 | 1.04 | 2.31 |
| Predicted ........ | 30 | 161.80 | 4.13 | 22.62 | 2.92 | | | |

## TABLE XXXIII

*Comparison of Actual and Predicted Scores on Special Spelling Test Given at Close of Fifteen-Week Experimental Period for Pupils in Lowest Fifth of Control Group. Prediction Based on Regression Education from Whole of Control Group*

| Lowest Fifth | No. of Cases | Mean | S. E.ᴍ | S. D. | S. E.σ | Difference in Means | S. E.Diff. M | Difference in Means / S. E.Diff. M |
|---|---|---|---|---|---|---|---|---|
| **Otis Test** | | | | | | | | |
| Actual ........... | 30 | 56.80 | 6.55 | 35.88 | 4.63 | −2.80 | 1.65 | 1.70 |
| Predicted ........ | 30 | 59.60 | 6.66 | 36.48 | 4.71 | | | |
| **Reading Test** | | | | | | | | |
| Actual ........... | 30 | 51.00 | 4.81 | 26.94 | 3.48 | −1.40 | 1.25 | 1.12 |
| Predicted ........ | 30 | 52.40 | 4.26 | 23.34 | 3.01 | | | |
| **Standard Spelling Test** | | | | | | | | |
| Actual ........... | 30 | 37.80 | 2.92 | 16.02 | 2.07 | −2.60 | .84 | 3.10 |
| Predicted ........ | 30 | 40.40 | 2.40 | 13.14 | 1.70 | | | |
| **Special Spelling Test** | | | | | | | | |
| Actual ........... | 30 | 34.60 | 1.39 | 7.59 | .98 | −4.50 | .46 | 9.78 |
| Predicted ........ | 30 | 39.10 | 1.04 | 5.70 | .74 | | | |

achieved less than was predicted and, in the case of the lowest fifth in general spelling ability and in the special spelling test, these differences in means are significant. In the experimental group, on the other hand, the lowest fifth selected on these same bases almost achieved the prediction, in one case, and exactly achieved it in the other. From these data it would appear that even the lowest group benefited from being taught under the experimental conditions.

It would be well at this point to summarize the findings with relation to the gains of the high and low groups. Some of the evidence is contradictory, largely because of comparisons made with the control group in which the number of cases was only thirty. The smallness of this sample is one cause of the seeming contradictory results obtained by the three methods which were used in comparing the gains of these groups.

The findings regarding the pupils in the highest fifth of the experimental groups are all consistent regardless of the method used in treating the data. Whether this upper fifth is selected on the basis of mental ability, of reading ability, of general spelling ability, or of achievement on the special spelling test, it shows similar results. The more able pupils not only gain more in the experimental group than they do in the control group, but they make gains which are considerably larger than for average students in the experimental group. It is the more able children, then, who benefit most from the experimental conditions.

For the children of low ability in intelligence, in reading ability, in spelling ability, and in achievement on the special spelling test, the evidence is not quite so clear. Because of the small number of cases perhaps the most reliable indication comes from a comparison of the means in which the standard error of the difference in means takes into account the small number of cases in the control group. This method indicated that the lowest fifth in mental ability gained about equally whether they were located in the control group or in the experimental group. For pupils in the lowest fifth of the group with respect to the other three factors there seems to be greater gains in the experimental group than in the control group, but these children do not gain as much from the experimental conditions as do the average children in the experimental group. When other methods were used in treating these data, it was indicated that there was little advantage for children of low ability whether they were in the control group or the experimental group. These findings should be taken with caution, however, because of the small number of cases involved in the control group. The safest conclusion is that the children of less ability do not gain as much advantage from membership in the experimental group as do brighter children, but that there is some advantage for them in the experimental conditions.

*The Relation of Gains to Various Measures.* Simple correlations between the actual gains made during the fifteen weeks of experiment and various measures of ability based upon the control group are presented in Table XXXIV. It will be noted from this table

TABLE XXXIV

*Correlations of Gains Between Test I and Test II*
*With Other Measures in County B (Control Group)*

|  | r |
| --- | --- |
| Chronological Age | −.123 |
| Word Meaning | .234 |
| Literature | .241 |
| Total Reading | .303 |
| Social Studies | .221 |
| Standard Spelling | .454 |
| Otis Test | .285 |
| Spelling Test I | .413 |
| Spelling Test II | .493 |
| Spelling Test III | .607 |

that the highest relationship is between the gains and the final scores made at the end of the fifteen weeks' period, $r = .607$. The second highest relationship exists between the scores made at the end of five weeks and the gains, $r = .493$. Of the remaining eight correlations between gains and scores obtained on the various measures which were available at the beginning of the experiment, the highest relationship is between the standard spelling test and the gains, $r = .454$. That this should be higher than the relationship between gains and scores on Spelling Test I, $r = .413$, is an indication that the general spelling test may be a better measure of the ability to learn the spelling of new words than is a test based only on new words.

Another interesting fact given in this table is that the gains are related more closely to the total reading score, $r = .303$, than to general mental ability, $r = .285$. This would seem to mean that the ability in reading is a better index of the learning of new words than brightness alone.

It should also be observed that scores in literature relate more closely to gains, $r = .241$, than do the word-meaning scores, $r = .234$. Likewise, the measure of social studies ability has the lowest relationship of any of the measures, $r = .221$, except chronological age, in spite of the fact that the experiment was carried on in a social studies situation. Chronological age, of course, had a negative correlation with the gains because in a single grade the older children tend to be those who have somewhat less ability than the younger children. The correlation between gains and chronological age was $- .123$.

*Summary.* The three experimental groups and the control group were found to be practically identical in means and standard deviations with relation to the score on the initial administration of the spelling test, the factor most closely related to the scores made on the final test. With regard to three other factors of fairly high relationship to the final scores, the experimental group is superior to the control group in reading and the control group is superior to the experimental group on the Otis test of mental ability and on the test of general spelling ability. The various groups are similar with regard to four other factors. In chronological age they vary from one to the other by only two months. In a general test of the social studies there are slight differences in means, and on a test of word meaning and literature the experimental group surpass the control group by small but significant amounts.

The results of the experiment were found to be as follows :

1. Each of the groups has an original mean score on the special spelling test indicating that the children could spell an

average of about 30 per cent of the words before the beginning of the experiment. Since they had never been taught these words, this indicates the fact of incidental learning of spelling of unusual words.

2. All groups gained significantly in ability to spell unusual words during five weeks and considerably more during the fifteen weeks although they had had no direct instruction in the spelling of these words.

3. Slight differences existed among the means on the special spelling test after the five weeks of the experiment, but in only one case is the difference statistically significant.

4. After the entire fifteen weeks of the experiment the three experimental groups showed similar means, but each of them made gains considerably greater than the gains made by the control group. These differences between each of the experimental groups and the control group are statistically significant.

5. Using the method of prediction it was found that each of the experimental groups made mean scores on the special spelling test considerably higher than was predicted on the basis of the achievement of the control group and all these differences are statistically significant. This indicates that the pupils in the experimental groups achieved more because of the experimental conditions than they would have achieved in the control group.

6. Pupils in the upper fifth in mental ability in the experimental group made much greater gains in ability to spell unusual words than the average students in this group.

7. Pupils in the upper fifth in reading ability in the experimental group made much greater gains in ability to spell unusual words than the average pupils in this group.

8. Pupils in the upper fifth in general spelling ability in the experimental group made much greater gains in ability to spell unusual words than the average pupils in this group.

9. Pupils in the upper fifth on the special spelling test in the experimental group made much greater gains in ability to spell unusual words than the average pupils in this group.

10. The lowest fifth in mental ability in the experimental group showed little evidence of the influence of the experimental con-

ditions. They gained about the same amount as similar children in the control group.

11. Pupils in the lowest fifth of the experimental group with respect to reading probably gained but little by being in the experimental group.

12. Pupils in the lowest fifth of the experimental group in general spelling ability did better in the experimental group than similar children in the control group but their gains were not as great as were the gains for average pupils in the experimental group.

13. Pupils in the lowest fifth of the experimental group on achievement on the special spelling test did better than similar children in the control group but their gains were not as great as were the gains for average pupils in the experimental group.

14. The scores made on a test of general spelling ability had a closer relationship to the gains made by pupils during the experiment than did their initial scores on the special spelling test. Their initial scores furnish a better basis of prediction of their final scores, but the general spelling scores afford a better basis for predicting gains.

15. The total reading score is a better index of gain than is general mental ability.

16. Scores on the literature test are somewhat more closely related to gains than are the scores on the word meaning test. Both correlations are relatively low, however.

17. Of the test scores, the measure of social studies achievement has lowest relationship to the gains in ability to spell these new social studies words.

# VI

## Summary, Conclusions, and Recommendations

THIS study was an investigation of a single type of secondary learning. "Secondary learning" was defined as the more or less unforeseen changes which take place in boys and girls as a result of school experiences—learning which takes place secondarily to the attainment of primary objectives. In this study the type of secondary learning investigated was acquiring the ability to spell certain unusual words which occur in relation to the field of social studies in the sixth grade in the two counties studied. By "unusual" is meant that the words whose learning was studied were those outside the 3,000 commonest words which constitute the spelling curriculum of the elementary school. It was proposed to discover whether boys and girls in the study would acquire the ability to spell certain uncommon words associated with their work in the social studies without the direct teaching of such words.

The problem was stated as follows: To discover the relationship of the teaching of certain units in social studies and of the teaching of history and geography separately to the ability of children to spell words peculiar to the units or subjects.

*Method of the Study.* Three equated experimental groups in the county teaching a single social studies course were selected. A group in a similar county in which geography and history were taught separately by a more traditional approach was then chosen as a control group and equated with the other three groups. The number of cases upon which there were complete data in each of the four groups ranged from 151 to 274.

Approximate equality from group to group was sought in the

type of communities, the economic level of the families of the children, administrative conditions in the schools, teachers' salaries, and professional preparation and ability of the teachers. Close similarity, if not equality, was secured in important measurable factors, such as initial scores in the special spelling test, achievement in a social studies test, age, intelligence, reading ability, and a test of general spelling ability. Slight differences which existed tended on the whole to favor the control group.

The experimental factor which differed from County A to County B was the organization and the teaching of the social studies. Equal amounts of time were devoted to this teaching in the two counties. In County B history and geography were taught separately by the textbook method and with narrow informational objectives. The groups in County A were taught a unified course in social studies with objectives of broader scope and the units which were taught involved a wider range of reading and a greater variety of learning activities than in County B. The three experimental groups differed from each other in the order in which three five-week units were taught during the fifteen weeks of the experiment. At the end of five weeks each experimental group had had a different unit, but at the end of fifteen weeks the three groups had covered the same three units, but in a different order.

The amount of secondary learning of unusual words peculiar to the units in social studies and the subjects of geography and history was measured by a special spelling test constructed from the unusual words occurring frequently in this social studies work. It was shown that the test was valid for this purpose and that it was highly reliable. The test was administered at the beginning of the experiment for purposes of equating; it was given again at the end of five weeks and repeated at the end of fifteen weeks. Its length and nature practically precluded the possibility of learning from the test alone. The method of testing was shown to be that which is commonly accepted and which has not been shown to be invalid by any studies yet made.

*Conclusions.* The results of the study are given in the summary on pages 105-107. What can be concluded from these results?

1. A unified treatment of social studies in the sixth grade involving wide reading and a great variety of learning activities results in a larger amount of secondary learning of spelling words than does a more traditional type of textbook teaching of history and geography. This was found true in each of the experimental groups when it was compared with the control group.

This gives reliable support for the hypothesis of modern educators that a learning situation results in the accomplishment of a variety of important objectives. It indicates that the same amount of time given to a subject of study can result in greater amounts of secondary learning of spelling when learning situations are varied than when ordinary textbook teaching is adhered to.

2. The study suggests that individual spelling vocabularies are acquired from pursuit of various activities relating to specialized fields. The children acquired additions to their individual spelling vocabularies of uncommon words because they pursued learning activities relating to the special topics of the units and the subjects. This was true for both the control and the experimental groups.

3. The wide range among the pupils in gains made in learning to spell the new words indicates that the techniques of learning to spell new words were acquired to varying degrees by the pupils. It bolsters up the contention of other investigators in the field of spelling that such techniques of learning to spell need to be taught to children. The fact that the gains have relatively low correlations with intelligence suggests that the acquiring of these techniques has been largely an individual matter and that it is responsible for the gains rather than intelligence or reading ability.

4. The fact that all the groups made average scores at the beginning of the experiment indicated that ability to spell about 30 per cent of the new words which they had never been taught can be attributed to one or both of two factors. Either they had learned these words in previous reading and other activities or they had learned enough generalizations about spelling to spell a considerable number of new words simply by applying these generalizations. Probably both factors were responsible, but it is reasonable to believe that the school can aid both by offering a wide and varied program of reading and other activities in connection with school

work and by teaching a few generalizations with regard to spelling which can be applied in a reasonably large proportion of the cases when attempting to spell new words.

5. The fact that there were only slight differences among the three experimental groups after five weeks of teaching different units suggests that the method rather than content of these units was responsible for the gains. The method in all three groups was fairly uniform: much reading, much writing, much discussion, as well as a variety of other activities. The content was totally different in the three units and we might have expected greater differences in incidental learning if the content were the sole factor.

6. This study confirms other studies comparing more modern methods with traditional methods of organizing and teaching in that it is the pupils of greater ability who seem to gain most from these more progressive methods. The fact, however, that even the students of lesser ability gained somewhat more under experimental conditions than in the control group suggests the value of a varied program even for these children. This is important because, in a skill usually considered a matter of drill, the freer conditions seemed better even for children of low ability.

7. The fact that the highest correlation between gains and the various tests given at the beginning of the experiment was the correlation between these gains and scores on a general spelling test indicates that such a test is a more valid index of the secondary learning of spelling of unusual words than is intelligence or any other factor which was measured. That this correlation was as low as .454, however, suggests that other factors are important. A teacher can use the children's achievement on a standard spelling test only as an extremely rough indication of the spelling which he may be expected to learn secondarily.

8. It is appropriate to formulate some hypotheses which will explain the fact that it was the pupils of greater ability in spelling, in reading, and in mental ability who profited most from the experimental conditions. It is reasonable to believe that the fact that they are in the upper fifth of the total group implies that they have pretty well mastered the abilities required in handling materials and making adequate use of them. The experimental conditions

involved greater exposure under freer conditions to reading materials and writing activities and pupils in the upper fifth were those who were most able to take advantage of them. In the control group the more able pupils who might have utilized a greater quantity of materials were not provided with them to as great an extent as in the experimental groups, nor were they working under conditions which permitted them to make as effective use of the materials they had. It is the author's belief that it is this exposure to materials when there is the ability to handle them that is responsible for the increase in the ability to spell unusual words. Therefore, it is clear that these pupils in the upper fifth could be expected to achieve much more secondary learning under the experimental conditions than pupils of equal ability under the more rigid conditions of the control group.

9. We can likewise speculate on the probable reasons that the pupils in the lower fifth in various abilities seem to have benefited so little more from the experimental conditions than did comparable students in the control group. There seem to be two alternatives. Either the teachers of the experimental groups were not able to arrange proper learning conditions which were appropriate for children in the lower fifth in spelling ability, reading ability, and mental ability or these children were so handicapped in their ability to handle reading materials and writing activities that they could not take advantage of freer conditions. They did as well and perhaps a little better under the experimental conditions, but they were so limited in these primary abilities that they could cover little more with a variety of materials than they could in textbooks. Probably both of these alternatives were actually operative in the situation, but it would seem desirable for teachers who are working under a unit plan with abundant materials to provide remedial work for children who are deficient in reading, spelling, and mental ability so that they are better able to handle the materials. Teachers ought, also, to experiment with special learning activities for this group which is less able.

*Recommendations for Further Investigation.* Numerous other gross studies of secondary learning need to be made. We need to know whether spelling ability is acquired secondarily in reading alone or whether the teaching of composition results in greater learning of this sort. Similarly, it should be determined whether specialized spelling vocabularies in science, in health, and in the arts are acquired through study of these fields without special stress upon spelling.

Gross studies are needed of secondary learning of other types, such as the learning of skills in handwriting through social studies instruction or through written composition.

Refined studies are needed to determine the precise factors responsible for secondary learning. While this investigation shows that these gains are related to the broad method and organization of the teaching of the social studies, it has not determined what particular activities are most fruitful in producing secondary learning. Was it the reading that developed the ability to spell? Was it the writing of numerous compositions related to the social studies? Was it class discussion of social studies questions? Careful studies utilizing the method of factor analysis should throw much light upon these problems.

In a recent article Horn has stressed the importance of studies of secondary, or what he calls "incidental" learning of spelling. He suggests some of the types of research which are needed[1]:

Before one can decide whether or not to reply wholly or even chiefly upon the incidental learning of spelling, such questions as the following must be answered: What are the activities or subjects in connection with which incidental learning occurs? What, or how much, is learned incidentally? How do the results obtained by purely incidental learning compare with those obtained by direct teaching? How feasible and economical is it from the standpoint of administration to provide for the incidental teaching of spelling? Even those who hold that spelling should be taught in a separate period cannot escape the necessity of inquiring into the degree to which spelling is learned outside the spelling period. Words which can safely be left to incidental learning may be omitted with profit from the spelling course of study. Moreover, words which are placed in regular spelling lists presumably will require much less review for maintenance if they are frequently written outside the spelling period. One of the most difficult problems in grading the course of study in spelling is to discover the degree to which spelling is motivated and practiced through the various uses which

[1] Horn, Ernest, "The Incidental Teaching of Spelling," *The Elementary English Review*, XIV (January, 1937), pp. 3-5.

are made of writing at each grade level, both in and out of school. Since there is undoubtedly some incidental learning of spelling through the reading and writing, and even in the speaking done in connection with other school subjects, it is very important to discover the nature and extent of such learning.

The fact that all of the groups in this investigation were learning to spell words without direct instruction raises a fundamental question regarding the common list of words which should be taught to all children. One assumption about such a basic list is that it represents the spelling needs of all children. This is certainly true of some of the most common words, but at what point does the vocabulary begin to include words which are not needed by all children, even though used frequently by most children? When does the factor of individual differences in interests begin to operate in terms of a specialized vocabulary? Is the common list 3,000 words, or 2,500, or 5,000? This study would indicate that reading and other learning activities relating to special interests will tend to develop the ability to spell words relating to these special interests, and that a special spelling period can be defended only in terms of the common spelling needs of all or at least nearly all individuals. Vocabulary research should determine, then, not only words occurring with greatest frequency in various sources, but also the percentage of adults and of children of various ages who utilize these words in normal writing situations. This will provide a sound basis for a general spelling vocabulary, and additional research will determine the extent to which specialized vocabularies can be developed secondarily through other types of learning situations.

# Bibliography

AIKIN, WILFORD M. "The Purpose of the Eight-Year Experimental Study." *Educational Record,* XVI (January, 1935), pp. 107-120.

BARKER, VILDA MADGE. "The Ability of Children Who Have Had Six Years of Training to Spell Words That Have Not Been Studied." Master's Thesis, College of Education, State University of Iowa, June, 1927.

BRUNER, HERBERT B. *The Place of Units in Course of Study Construction.* South Dakota Curriculum Revision Program, Bulletin No. 2, State Department of Education, Pierre, South Dakota, 1930. 22 p.

CARROLL, HERBERT ALLEN. *Generalization of Bright and Dull Children; A Comparative Study with Special Reference to Spelling.* Bureau of Publications, Teachers College, Columbia University, New York, 1930. 54 p.

COMPTON, LILLIAN. "The Social Studies in the Elementary School." *Curriculum Revision Program, Allegany County, Maryland.* Allegany County Public Schools, Cumberland, Maryland, 1930. (mimeographed).

COOK, WALTER WELLMAN. *The Measurement of General Spelling Ability Involving Controlled Comparisons Between Techniques.* University of Iowa, Studies in Education, Vol. VI, No. 6. The University Press, Iowa City, February 15, 1932. 112 p.

FORAN, T. G. *The Form of Spelling Tests.* Educational Research Bulletins, The Catholic University of America, Vol. IV, No. 8 (October, 1929), The Catholic Education Press, Washington, D. C. 24 p.

GATES, ARTHUR I. *Reading for Public School Administrators.* Bureau of Publications, Teachers College, Columbia University, New York, 1931. 126 p.

GUILER, WALTER S. "Validation of Methods of Testing Spelling." *Journal of Educational Research,* XX (October, 1929), pp. 181-189.

HORN, ERNEST. "The Incidental Teaching of Spelling." *The Elementary English Review,* XIV (January, 1937), pp. 3-5.

PEARSON, HENRY CARR AND HENRY SUZZALLO. *Essentials of Spelling, Middle Grades.* American Book Company, New York, 1921. 84 p.

PINTNER, R., RINSLAND, H. D., AND ZUBIN, J. "The Evaluation of Self-Administering Spelling Tests." *Journal of Educational Psychology,* XX (February, 1929), pp. 107-111.

SIFERT, EARL R. "A Comparative Study of the Abilities of Eighth Grade Children to Spell Studied and Unstudied Words." Master's Thesis, College of Education, State University of Iowa, August, 1926.

THOMPSON, ROBERT S. *The Effectiveness of Modern Spelling Instruction.* Bureau of Publications, Teachers College, Columbia University, New York, 1930. 81 p.

THORNDIKE, EDWARD L. *The Teacher's Word Book.* Bureau of Publications, Teachers College, Columbia University, New York, 1921. 134 p.

THORNDIKE, EDWARD L. *Teacher's Word Book of 20,000 Words.* Bureau of Publications, Teachers College, Columbia University, New York, 1931. 182 p.

TYLER, RALPH W. "Evaluation: A Challenge to Progressive Education." *Educational Research Bulletin,* XIV (January 16, 1935), pp. 9-16.

WRIGHTSTONE, J. WAYNE. *Appraisal of Experimental High School Practices.* Bureau of Publications, Teachers College, Columbia University, New York, 1936. 194 p.

WRIGHTSTONE, J. WAYNE. *Appraisal of Newer Elementary School Practices.* Bureau of Publications, Teachers College, Columbia University, New York, 1938. 221 p.

# Vita

I. KEITH TYLER was born at Table Rock, Nebraska, February 18, 1905. He attended elementary schools in Peru, Hastings, and Crete, Nebraska, and was graduated in the spring of 1921 from Lincoln High School, Lincoln, Nebraska. His undergraduate work was taken at the University of Nebraska where he received the Bachelor of Arts degree in 1925.

His graduate work included a year at the Yale Divinity School, a year at the Union Theological Seminary, and two and a half years at Teachers College, Columbia University. He was granted the Master of Arts degree from the latter institution in 1930. He was Naomi Norsworthy Fellow at Teachers College, for the year 1930-31. He became a member of Kappa Delta Pi and Phi Delta Kappa while attending Teachers College.

Mr. Tyler is the author of numerous articles in the fields of the curriculum and radio education and of *High School Students Talk It Over*, a verbatim account of a series of discussions by high school students which he conducted over the Ohio School of the Air in 1936. He is one of the editors of the *News Letter*, a monthly publication bringing information to the teacher about the radio, the motion picture and the press. For three years he was senior editor of the *Ohio Radio Announcer*, a monthly bulletin listing recommended radio programs for educational use and containing articles on the school utilization of radio programs. He is also national radio chairman of the American Federation of Teachers.